ASIAN WAYS

A Westerner's Guide to
Asian Business Etiquette

NICK FRENCH

AARDVARK
PRESS

Aardvark Press Publishing (Pty) Ltd, PO Box 37571, Valyland 7978, South Africa

www.aardvarkpress.co.za

This book was printed in South Africa,
on paper that was produced from managed forests.

ISBN 978-0-9584907-5-7

www.asian-ways.com

Design and setting by Orchard Publishing
Front cover photograph © Nick French
Back cover photograph © David Sparrow
Cover design by Orchard Publishing
Printed by Interpak, 22 Willowton Road, Pietermaritzburg, South Africa

Contents

Each country treatment includes:
- Country background (population, ethnicity and religion, language and script, regional structures, political environment)
- Religious, cultural and historial influences
- Local customs and etiquette
- Preparation and awareness
- Meeting formalities
- Meals and entertainment

Preface

In the Asian business environment, interpersonal relationships play a significant role, far more so than in the West. Appropriate Asian etiquette is necessary for both relationship development and future chances of business success.

Visitors to Asia often return home after short trips, believing that they have been steeped in Asian culture and claiming to be the foremost authorities on local customs. How wrong they are! These cultures are so rich, diverse and complex that one simply cannot learn and assimilate their detailed intricacies in a short period of time. Achieving proficiency in Asian customs takes time and effort. For newcomers to the Asian environment (such as businesspeople about to travel to Asian countries for the first time) this book serves as a useful reference for proper conduct. Regular travellers around the region, wishing to improve their competency in Asian customs, will also find this book a valuable tool.

This guide highlights the most important facets of etiquette in a number of Asian countries. The reader will be able to easily access the most important "need-to-know" items, and put them to use with minimum effort. This volume is small enough to be slipped into a briefcase for use as a convenient reference, while travelling within the Asian region.

There are some customs that are common to many Asian countries. Part I deals with these generic principles, so that the reader can attain a good level of basic understanding at an early stage. This provides a good starting platform for visiting any Asian country, which can be supplemented with the country- specific recommendations presented in Part II. Part II also contains information about country demographics, history and religious influences, providing a useful background to cultural origins. By reading this book, business travellers will be able to improve their Asian intercultural skills with ease, and apply these to good effect in both their business and social lives.

PART I

Asian intercultural competence

1 Introduction

Towards better intercultural competence

Congratulations! In selecting this book, and reading this first paragraph, you have already demonstrated a desire to improve your conduct in the Asian world. Whether you visit the Orient for business or pleasure, there is no doubt that experiences and achievements will be richer and more rewarding when one is sensitised to the customs of the region. By going one step further and implementing appropriate behaviour, the rewards will be even greater. Without doubt, this book will lead you along the path to success. Good luck!

The need to adapt

Despite the apparent wave of westernisation that is sweeping across the East, as evidenced by the explosion of American and European fast-food chains, coffee shops and supermarkets, the basic tenets of local Eastern culture remain intact. Unfortunately, foreigners tend to forget this and assume that local values and customs are also becoming more westernised. While to some extent this may be true, the process is slow, meaning that grass-root, traditional Eastern values continue to prevail. As global trade continues to expand, and business encounters between East and West increase, there is a growing need for businessmen to be interculturally competent.

Respect, understanding and the practice of intercultural sensitivity in both business and social dealings add a new dimension and challenge to achieving personal goals in Asia. This could be to clinch a $100-million dollar deal with a Chinese state-owned company, or simply to receive better service from a shop assistant in Thailand.

Asians believe in the importance of building a firm personal relationship before proceeding with business. This is contrary to the western view that personal relationships only begin once a business deal has been concluded. One important aspect of the Asian relationship-building process is gaining credibility, as generally Asians are less trusting than westerners. Trust barriers tend to be higher across an East–West intercultural divide. Developing relationships obviously takes time, requiring patience and tolerance. One method of accelerating this process is to move away from usual western norms and adapt to the local Asian culture.

Why East and West are different

Why are East and West so different in their ways? Over time, their cultures have been shaped differently, with religious and other teachings as contributing factors. This can be traced back to the fact that western ideals emanate from Europe, while those of Asia originate from China and the Middle East.

The western religious backgrounds of Christianity and Judaism focus on the tenets of the Old and New Testaments in the Bible, that define certain ideals. Many of the customs in existence throughout Asia are derived from the ancient Chinese culture that has spread across the entire Asian region. People often underestimate how much underlying Chinese culture prevails in many south-east Asian countries (such as the Philippines, Indonesia and Thailand), despite the dominance of other ethnic groups. Chinese traits can be traced back to Taoist and Confucian philosophies, both of which emanated from China before the birth of Christ. These teachings emphasise the need for the preservation of harmony, including the need to maintain healthy relationships between individuals. Great importance is also placed on family values. Over the centuries, these principles have spread throughout Asia as the Chinese migrated to other countries in the vicinity. Although the local religions of these countries espouse differing beliefs, the underlying effects of Chinese customs continue to be ingrained in their specific cultures. A deeper insight as to how the dominant religions and philosophies of Asia contribute towards local behaviour and etiquette is provided in Chapter 3.

It's all about attitude

Before embarking on a programme of improving intercultural competence, a self-assessment should be made. To successfully implement the various facets of Asian etiquette, a change of attitude is necessary. Westerners, particularly those who have not lived in Asia, believe that their cultures are superior to those of the East. Hence, when they arrive in an Asian country, their manner and approach does not change – in fact, they expect the locals to bend towards their "superior" ways. Such an approach will not take the errant visitor very far. A change in mindset or a humbler approach is clearly indicated.

Firstly, any feeling of superiority over the Asian people should be replaced by a more respectful attitude, which will no doubt occur when you become immersed in these fascinating cultures.

Secondly, it will be necessary to become educated in, and attuned to, the ways of the Asian world. **Awareness of the need to develop and foster harmonious relationships is absolutely essential.**

Finally, three key words that should be part of any Asian visitor's dictionary are "courtesy", "tolerance" and "patience". There will be many times when the Asian system will give rise to frustration. In such situations aggressive behaviour, or loss of temper, may result in dire consequences.

Women in business in Asia

The businesswoman's ability to succeed in some countries may be compromised by her gender, particularly in marketing, sales or business-development environments, where personal relationships are key. Acceptance of western women in the Asian business environment varies across the countries. For instance, business in Japan and Korea is highly male-dominated. Surprisingly, in the Islamic countries of Malaysia and Indonesia, where a higher degree of male dominance would be expected, a significant proportion of women exist in higher echelons of business.

What can western women do in Asia, in order to overcome cultural barriers from a disadvantaged position? As discouraging as it may seem for those with strong beliefs about equality in the workplace, women with outgoing personalities should assume a more reserved demeanour. As there can be some initial prejudice from Asian males (which might not be outwardly apparent), it will take longer to form a solid business relationship, requiring additional patience and tenacity. In Japan and Korea, senior women executives will have to pay extra attention to demonstrating their seniority through the local etiquette protocols, otherwise they may be mistaken for junior staff, with little decision-making authority.

Asian culture is not an exact science

Although so-called "generic rules" of appropriate behaviour can be defined, there are many local variations. With the increase in East–West contact, there is no doubt that many younger Asians are becoming more westernised and less observant of their own traditional cultures. Hence westerners may find it easier to deal with younger generations, while greater effort will be required to comply with the traditional beliefs of older Asians. There may also be diverging opinions between local inhabitants as to how regional customs should be observed and, in some cases, these are open to interpretation.

Going forward

The next chapter gives a thorough overview of aspects of customs and etiquette that are common to most countries in Asia. This should be seen as a conditioning exercise for altering attitudes and conforming to Asian ways. Significant benefits will be gained by simply reading Chapter 2. In order to gain a deeper insight, however, study of the country-specific chapters in Part II is recommended.

2 Generic principles of Asian etiquette

Asian intercultural competence requires sensitivity to the cultural and behavioural differences between East and West, thus enabling effective relationships to be developed. There are a number of generic principles of behaviour that are applicable in the Asian business world that can be categorised as follows:

- Mindset.
- Planning and preparation.
- Appropriate behaviour.
- Business interaction.
- Entertainment.

Mindset

As a first step towards improving Asian relationship skills, the principal differences between the outlooks of East and West should be understood. There are four linked factors that dominate the way most Asians think and operate in their day-to-day dealings. These may not necessarily have the same level of importance in all countries, but they all contribute in one way or another:

- Interpersonal relationships.
- Trust and respect.
- Saving face.
- Group importance.

Interpersonal relationships

Asians tend to evaluate how well they relate to people with whom they work or socialise by a "feeling of the stomach". In the USA and Europe, relationships are seen as flowing from business transactions, and may only begin to flourish once business has actually been concluded. Asians do not perceive relationship development as a result of such processes, but rather as a primary and integral part of it. Business will not commence until a satisfactory relationship is in place. For westerners, this adds an interesting dimension and challenge to doing business in the East.

Unfortunately relationship-building takes time, necessitating more frequent contact over longer time frames than in a western context. In Asia, after-hours socialising is used to a greater extent as a tool for bonding. To this end, it is advisable to accept invitations to after-hours functions, such as dinners and cocktail parties, not to mention some of the more interesting forms of entertainment that might be suggested. Much can also be gained by extending similar invitations to your Asian counterparts.

Trust and respect

By nature, Asians are not trusting people. Circles of trust are normally limited to close-knit family units. For instance, when meeting a member of their own culture for the first time, Chinese people take time to establish common ground. Those coming from the same part of China or speaking the same dialect are more readily accepted. As can be imagined, westerners are not so easily welcomed. It stands to reason that levels of trust will only increase once a healthy relationship has been established. Conduct of a devious manner will create suspicion and should be avoided at all times. This could harm the level of trust and hence damage not only the relationship, but also the chances of future commercial success. Westerners should therefore act in a responsible, consistent and committed manner at all times.

Asians in general show higher levels of reverence to people of age and seniority. This means that older, more senior western executives will command greater attention and respect when visiting Asia.

Saving face

The need to save face in compromising situations is quite common throughout the world, but even more so in Asia. A Japanese emperor was once quoted as saying: "To lose face is to lose everything. To lose everything is not necessarily to lose face."

Responses and actions in Asia may be governed by the need either to save one's own face or give face to another person. Asians may carry out seemingly irrational actions in order to save face. When an answer to a question is not known, or conflict is imminent, an oblique response may be given. It would be losing face to admit that an answer cannot be provided. Here are specific examples of how Asians might react in potentially face-losing situations:

- Japanese have a great reluctance to convey negative responses by directly saying "No", or "This will be difficult". Such an answer may cause loss of face to the recipient of such news. A "grey" answer may be given, the real meaning of which will only become clear from ensuing actions (or lack thereof).
- Malays might reluctantly agree to an issue that they have difficulty in accepting, and later follow their preference anyway.
- Thais have an even better way of avoiding face-losing situations – they merely smile and hope a confrontation will go away!

Group importance

One of the key differences in behaviour between East and West is attitude towards individualism. In the West, individual performance is recognised and encouraged; in Asia, there is greater respect for group and team performance. For this reason, an individual presenting an aggressive egotistical front will not be well received. Whereas in the West, delegation of authority in decision-making is permitted, Asians consider group consultation more important. Thus, in certain Asian countries, decision-making does not happen quickly – patience is required!

Preparation and planning

Before embarking on a trip to Asia ensure that you possess the tools of the business trade. Spending a little extra time and effort on preparation can prevent embarrassing situations, while also providing an opportunity to create a favourable impression.

Business cards and promotional literature

Business or calling cards, also known in Asia as "name cards", command respect and should be handled with more care than they are in the West. It may be necessary to have name cards translated into the language of the country being visited, particularly in the case of China, Korea and Japan. The recommended way is to have one side of the card printed in English, and the other side in the foreign text. Caution should be taken to confirm how a western name appears when translated. During translation into pictorial or phonetic scripts, the exact pronunciation of a name may be altered slightly, leading to an offensive interpretation.

A large number of cards should be available, as meetings in Asia tend to have many attendees. It is always preferable to offer a crisp clean card. Cards should therefore be kept in a separate, good-quality name cardholder, to prevent them from becoming bent or dog-eared. A useful cardholder is one that has at least two pockets, one for the owner's cards, and the other in which collected cards can be placed.

In the event that corporate literature is being used to extensively promote a company or its product in an Asian country, it is advisable (but not essential) to have this translated as well. As with personal names, when translating a company or brand name into a foreign language, care should be exercised to ensure that the local interpretation of western words does not create undesirable inferences.

Executive essentials

The Chinese community throughout Asia evaluates a businessperson according to the brand of watch he or she is wearing. Expensive brands, particularly Rolex and higher quality Swiss-made watches, accord the wearer a high status. Selection of a respectable brand of watch is therefore suggested, particularly for more senior executives. This rule also applies to pens (Mont Blanc seems to be the preferred brand) as well as owning the latest technology in mobile phones.

Asians are prolific takers of photographs. Group photographs tend to be copied and distributed among participants. For instance, at a meal, an Asian associate may produce a camera and request all present to pose for a group photograph, as a souvenir of the occasion. Invariably, the western participant will receive a copy of the photograph at some future point. Insignificant as this may seem, it brings with it an opportunity to strengthen relationships. A camera can therefore be used to good advantage during group occasions to take photographs, copies of which should be distributed to all participants.

Crossing language barriers

Depending on which countries are to be visited and the calibre of people being met, it may be necessary to hire an interpreter. This is especially recommended when highly technical matters are going to be discussed.

If the Asian party comprehends English well and an interpreter is brought to the meeting, offence and mistrust could ensue. A way of reducing this risk is to involve the commercial section of a home country embassy or high commission. These institutions normally have marketing officers of local origin, whose responsibility it is to develop business relations between concerns in the foreign and host country. Local diplomatic marketing officers are usually more readily accepted as interpreters. It is recommended that time be spent beforehand in briefing the interpreter about company background, as well as the objective of the forthcoming meeting. Apart from the fact that the services of such "in-house" interpreters should be free (excluding their travel expenses), they can also be used as guides to reach appointments at addresses that are difficult to find. This benefit is useful in countries such as Japan, Korea and China, where outside main city centres the signage is often in local script, with no English translation to be seen.

In a sales and marketing environment, it may be necessary to engage either an agent or distributor to facilitate not only communication with end-customers, but also to handle commercial aspects of the business. Selection of suitable candidates can be a difficult process. Key selection criteria should entail the agent's ability to manage relationships across the East–West cultural gap. Become acquainted with likely agents before making any firm commitment.

Gifts

In Asia, gift giving, particularly from suppliers and service providers to clients is very common. Westerners should also follow this custom. While this may seem a fairly straightforward exercise, in some cultures, particularly those of Korea and China, a gift is presented to signify that advance favours may be requested.

Gifts should be of reasonable quality and aesthetically wrapped in crisp and clean paper. Care should be taken to ensure that the wrapping is not damaged during transportation of a gift. If necessary, gifts can be wrapped on arrival in a city by the business centre of a hotel. As it may be necessary to dispense a large number of gifts, where possible these should be limited to small, easy-to-pack items.

To be absolutely safe, the following basic rules regarding selection of gifts should be followed:

- A clock should not be given as a gift to a Chinese person. This is a sign that the recipient's time is up and death is imminent. Watches may be given as gifts, but to be absolutely safe these should also be avoided.
- Knives, scissors, letter-openers or other sharp cutting tools are also taboo, as they signal the severance of a relationship.
- Handkerchiefs and socks are also not recommended. For the Chinese these are associated with funerals.

- In some countries, attention to the type, number and colour of flowers to be given is important, as there may be protocols that should be observed.
- Gifts should not be wrapped in dark purple, white or black. These colours are associated with funerals in certain regions.
- It stands to reason that in an Islamic country, alcohol and products of pigs should not be given to Muslims.
- Articles manufactured from leather, such as wallets, key rings or purses, should not be given to Indians of Hindu belief, as they consider cows to be sacred.

It is preferable not to present an expensive gift (such as a bottle of whisky) to the most senior person at the meeting, while at the same time distributing smaller gifts to the more junior members of the group. If there is a need to show respect to more senior people, a more expensive gift can be presented in private. However, with increasing sensitivity to bribery, care should be exercised in this regard. It is considered rude to present a gift to only one person in a group, unless the gift can be shared.

Gifts are normally presented with both hands and a slight bow, showing a degree of humility. The receiver will not open a gift in front of the giver, as this is considered a sign of greed. Asian custom also dictates that this is not done, in case the receiver is disappointed by the gift and as a result of seeing this, the giver loses face. Westerners should therefore also postpone opening any gifts they receive from Asians, until later.

Dress code

For business meetings in Asia, a conservative business suit is suitable for men, and for ladies, similar attire of a conservative nature. Short skirts should not be worn. Women should note that in Japan and Korea it is considered formal to sit on the floor for meals. Appropriate attire should therefore be worn to facilitate getting up and down elegantly. For more formal occasions and when meeting senior clients, a dark suit is preferable. In certain countries in south-east Asia, such as Singapore and Malaysia, a jacket is not required. Although these tropical countries have hot climates, a short-sleeved shirt, even with a tie, is not recommended as this is considered casual.

There may be times when western visitors will be called upon to visit a temple, factory, house or restaurant, where shoes must be removed before entering. These are normally left outside and the visitor enters the room, donning slippers that are provided at the door. On these occasions, it is advisable to wear shoes that can be easily slipped on or off, rather than lace-ups. It stands to reason that old socks with holes in them should not be worn!

Meals

Eating utensils other than a knife and fork are used for the majority of Asian meals. In most cases chopsticks (Singapore, Japan, Korea and, of course, China), or a spoon and fork (Malaysia, Indonesia, Thailand and the Philippines) will be encountered.

Visitors to Asia should be reasonably proficient in the use of chopsticks, and to this end pre-visit practice is recommended – learning to pick up peanuts is a good way to start! While most restaurants will offer a knife and fork to a westerner struggling with chopsticks, it is best to avoid this embarrassment as it comes with a loss of face.

In Asian restaurants, soup may be served during the early part of a meal. It is consumed concurrently with other dishes as the meal progresses. Rice or noodles may only appear near the end of the meal, as "fillers" for those who are still hungry. There will be occasions when local menus containing unpalatable dishes will be served. It is considered good etiquette to partake of these, no matter how distasteful the food may seem. On no account should any distaste be displayed.

Appropriate behaviour

There are several "do's and don'ts" that can be applied across the whole of Asia. Recognition and implementation of these will stand visiting westerners in good stead:

Facial expressions and displays of anger

Asians tend not to show emotions and reactions by means of facial expression. They are also quite adept at observing and interpreting minor changes in the facial expressions of others. This is particularly relevant during negotiation, where non-verbal clues can be unintentionally imparted. It is advisable that westerners maintain a stoic expression, especially when surprised or annoyed.

Although Asians tend not to show emotion through facial expressions, some become flushed around the throat and neck when angered or under stress.

Body language

Asians consider certain postures commonly exhibited by westerners as aggressive. Good examples of this are the "hands on hips" pose displayed when queuing or waiting to be served, and the "folding of arms across the chest" during a confrontation. When sitting in a chair at a formal meeting, men should keep both feet on the floor. Their legs should not be crossed in such a way that the soles of the feet are pointing at anyone else. It is, however, permissible for ladies to cross their legs.

In some Asian countries where meals are taken sitting on the floor, it is important to sit in a manner where your feet are not pointed at any of the other diners. It is therefore necessary to sit either cross-legged, or with your legs tucked to one side pointing behind you.

Pointing and gesticulating

Although pointing with the finger is sometimes accepted in the East, this should be restricted. For instance, pointing at a person with the index finger should be avoided. A more acceptable form is using an open hand with the fingers together.

In Asia, the western way of beckoning a person by turning the palm of the hand upwards and motioning with a crooked index finger is considered offensive, as it portrays contempt. The Asian technique of inverting the hand so that the palm faces downwards, keeping the fingers together and flapping the hand up and down (similar to scooping out sand on the beach) is preferable.

Clicking of fingers

Clicking the thumb and middle finger to make a point during conversation or to summon a person, such as a waiter in a restaurant, is seen as demeaning and should therefore be avoided.

Touching and displays of affection

Although Asian personal body space is less than that of westerners, this does not imply that they are receptive to touching. The American manner of touching people on the shoulder when making a point, or putting an arm around the shoulder, is taboo. This applies even more so between genders. Any public displays of affection, such as hugging or kissing, should be avoided. In social situations, such as an informal dinner function, the European custom of kissing the hostess on departure is not practised.

Some Buddhist religions, particularly those of Thailand and Indochina, dictate that the head of a person, even that of a child, is considered most sacred and therefore should not be touched. Westerners should not be tempted to touch the head of an adorable looking youngster. As some Chinese, Korean and Japanese people also practise Buddhism, it is wise to observe this rule as standard practice throughout the whole region.

Clearing the nose

Westerners should recognise that in Asia it is perfectly normal not to blow a runny nose. Sniffing and hawking of phlegm is widely accepted. Loud nose blowing and sneezing, as practised in the West, can be highly offensive.

Accepting and paying compliments

It is a good practice to pass favourable comments to Asians regarding their personal and/or business accomplishments, as this is "giving face". However, an acknowledgement such as "Thank you" may not be well received. Such a response conveys a feeling of superiority. Instead, a humble response will be given or credit passed to others, with replies such as "Actually it was the team that did this", "We tried hard" etc. Westerners, when receiving compliments from Asians, should therefore not follow the usual custom of saying "Thank you", but rather endeavour to acknowledge the compliment in a more humble way.

Jokes, colloquialisms and double meanings

Oriental humour is different from that of the West, and in most cases jokes of western origin are not comprehended. In the Asian environment, westerners should refrain from telling jokes or using any play on words in presentations – this could cause misunderstandings and embarrassment. Colloquialisms (for example, the phrase "The shoe is on the other foot") will be confusing to Asians.

Discussion topics

Some westerners commit a fatal error by assuming that it is safe to criticise one Asian group in the presence of another. Owing to the considerable amount of movement of the various Asian nationalities across borders, it is better not to pass opinions relating to political, religious and cultural matters.

Asians are inclined to ask seemingly direct personal questions during early stages of an acquaintance. This is not considered bad manners to them. Offence should not be shown – diversionary answers can be given if necessary.

Group vs. individual

In business discussions and correspondence, the pronouns and possessives "we", "us" and "our" rather than "I", "me" and "my" should be used by representatives of a team or company.

Family values

Asians place great importance on family life and having children. They can be quite inquisitive about family background – much more so than the average westerner might anticipate. In Asia, it is considered important for married couples to have children, failing which they are seen as lacking.

Admiring possessions

Open admiration of the personal possessions of others, when visiting Asian offices or homes, should be avoided. In some cultures the owner may feel obliged to offer the object as a gift.

Business interaction

The following protocols apply to business situations in the Asian environment:

Names and forms of address

The correct use of a person's name and form of address is important to create the right impression, during both initial and subsequent meetings.

In many Asian countries, the structure of people's names is different with regard to the order of given and family names. For instance, in the Chinese and Korean environments the family name appears first. During the early stages of a relationship, as in the West, people are addressed by their family names. Given names are only used as the relationship develops. However, in countries such as Japan and Korea, family names are used for longer periods (sometimes indefinitely) into the acquaintance. Conversely, in some south-east Asian countries (Thailand, Indonesia, Malaysia and Singapore) it is considered quite acceptable to use given names at an early stage.

Although in most cases it is acceptable to call Asians "Mr", "Ms" or "Mrs" as a form of address, there are also local forms of these titles. Use of the local term is well appreciated, and always creates a good impression. Detailed descriptions of these are provided in the country-specific chapters.

Meeting and greeting

There are certain protocols that apply to greeting Asian people in their home countries. Any effort to follow the local customs definitely curries favour. The normal manner of shaking hands between men is usually well accepted, although there are regional differences as to how this function is performed.

When meeting an Asian for the first time, one of the most important introductory processes is the exchange of name cards, and how this is executed. As described earlier, name cards have more status in Asia than in the West. They are considered to be an extension of the owner, and should therefore be treated with a high degree of respect. A card should not be defaced, bent or written on in the presence of the giver. Once a name card has been received, it should be studied and handled carefully. On no account should any comment on peculiarities regarding the owner's name be made, as this might cause embarrassment.

When presenting a name card, it should be removed from its holder and passed across with the side printed in the local script (if applicable) face up and the right way round, so that the recipient can read the card without having to rotate it. It should be handed over with a degree of formality, and not casually presented or flung across the table, as is sometimes done in western circles. If a meeting is scheduled after introductions have taken place, the received cards can be kept on the table and aligned with the seating positions of their owners. Once a meeting has been concluded, received name cards should not be placed in the back trouser pocket, as this is considered an insult.

Meeting formalities

Certain protocols apply to meeting formalities in Asia. The most senior member of a delegation should enter a meeting room first. There is also a rule as to where visitors should sit in a meeting venue. Guests are normally shown to the position of importance at the back of the room, facing the door, so that they can see who enters and leaves the room. In cases where there is a pleasant view from the room, this custom may be dispensed with and guests seated so as to enjoy the scenery. The most senior member of a business team should sit in the middle. Meeting rooms are normally the same as those encountered in the West, where facilities for visual presentations are available. An exception to this is in Japan, where for important guests a lounge setting may be selected, with comfortable chairs situated around a coffee table.

Meeting protocol

The following points are applicable to Asian meetings:

First meetings

In western environments, expectations are that decisions are made and deals concluded quickly. In the East, this is seldom achievable, particularly during the initial stages of the relationship-building phase. Sometimes first meetings with Asians can be limited to the exchange of company data and general introductions, without actually getting down to discussing specific business issues.

Style of speech

Depending on the English competency of the party with whom negotiations are being held, it is advisable to speak slowly and clearly. Even when using an interpreter, it is still necessary to speak slowly and pause at reasonable intervals to allow the interpreter time to assemble the contents of sentences and to translate them. Colloquialisms, phrases with double meanings and jokes should be avoided.

Periods of silence

Asians are used to long periods of silence during discussions. They do not feel obliged to keep a conversation moving. Such intervals are used for reflection and thought. Under such circumstances, westerners should not feel pressured to break the silence by speaking unnecessarily.

Evasive responses

During discussion periods, Asians may be asked a question to which they may not know the answer. Normal western ways would permit a frank and honest admission of ignorance. In Asia, such an admission would be seen as a loss of face and therefore an obtuse or diversionary answer may be given.

One should be aware of the mistaken "Yes". In many countries, a vague response can be interpreted with a positive bias, when in fact a strong negative message is implied. Answers such as "We'll think about it" or "This might be difficult" are intended to mean a strong "No" rather than a vague "Yes".

Negotiation style

When discussing commercial matters such as price, Asians have an uncanny knack of being able to negotiate aggressively. While westerners like to push for a quick resolution, Asians are more patient in this regard and use time as a tool to wear their western opposition down. At least two or three successive requests for concessions should be anticipated. Face may also be given to the other party by granting them a concession during a negotiation.

Written contracts

In some Asian countries there are aversions to signing lengthy contractual agreements. Apart from the fact that it may be difficult to understand western legal jargon, Asian cultures operate in such a way that a verbal "gentleman's agreement" is usually honoured. If any unforeseen problematic issue arises during the term of the agreement, this is settled by constructive negotiation. Even if an Asian signs an agreement, it is still possible that the terms therein may not be adhered to. Despite the existence of an ironclad agreement, frequent approaches may be made for changes or variances to contractual terms. It is advisable to anticipate such situations, and where possible to be flexible in acceding to such requests. In China and other developing Asian regions, it may also be difficult to legally enforce contractual terms that have been contravened.

Departing

It is normal for Asian hosts to escort guests to the lift lobby and bid them farewell, waiting until they have departed. It is recommended that this practice be followed whenever westerners are acting as hosts to visiting Asians.

Entertainment

Asians rely heavily on entertainment as a means of relationship-building under less formal circumstances. For this purpose, westerners are advised to take advantage of invitations to after-hours functions.

Meal invitations

After a meeting, an impromptu invitation for lunch or dinner may be extended. Where possible this should be accepted, as refusal may result in some loss of face to the host. If it is not possible to accept, an alternate time should be suggested.

Venues

After-hours entertainment in Asia can be the usual dinner, or something more "exotic", for example a visit to a hostess or Karaoke bar. It is advisable to be prepared for invitations to such types of entertainment and to accept them, as it is here that business relations can be truly advanced.

Unlike most western environments, entertainment at the home of an Asian host for business or social occasions is rare. Invariably home entertainment in Asia is reserved for family and close friends. Residences can be located quite some distance from places of work and in some countries, such as Japan, are simply too small for hosting. It is therefore more practical and convenient to entertain in the city.

Seating arrangements

Depending on the size of the group or the formality of the occasion, a private room off to one side of the main restaurant may be reserved. The most important diners (the senior host and guest) will be seated facing the entrance to the room. The most senior guest will usually be seated to the right of the most senior host, contrary to the custom in the West where they will be seated to the left.

In Japan and Korea, it is considered more formal to sit on the floor. While this is quite comfortable for Asian people, it may not necessarily suit westerners. For westerners suffering from orthopaedic problems, where getting up and down off the floor is problematic, it is acceptable to request that for health reasons, normal chairs are used. Such requests should be made well in advance, so that seating arrangements can be changed timeously. In most cases such a request will be acceded to without loss of face. Ladies should obviously wear attire that will allow them to sit elegantly and comfortably in such situations. If a meal is taken where floor seating is selected, it will be necessary that shoes be removed before entering the dining area. Should there be a need to visit the restroom during the meal, special slippers will be provided just outside the main eating area.

Table manners

Meal etiquette varies across the region, and from country to country. It is essential, however, to be proficient in the use of chopsticks, and with the Asian way of eating with a fork and spoon.

The following aspects of chopstick etiquette should be noted:

- Chopsticks should not be used like a knife and fork, so not separated into the left and right hand.
- Morsels of food should not be speared with a single chopstick. It is, however, acceptable to spike a difficult piece using both chopsticks held in one hand.
- Pointing or gesticulating with chopsticks should be avoided.
- Chopsticks should not be crossed when placed on the table. They should be placed side by side on the rest provided. If no chopstick rest has been provided, they can be placed on the table itself or resting together over a plate.
- Chopsticks should not be poked into a bowl of food and left standing up vertically in a soup bowl. This is only done at funerals, and is considered a sign of death.
- Chopsticks should not be dropped on the floor – this is considered bad luck. If this should happen, they should be replaced.
- Sometimes, as a sign of respect, a host will select a special morsel from a shared dish on the table and place it in the bowl or plate of a guest. This is a gesture of honour, and should be accepted with appreciation. Although not always practised, the giver should reverse his chopsticks and pick up the piece with the other end of his sticks – the thicker end. This is supposed to be more hygienic, as the thin ends come into contact with the mouth when eating.

Adapting to the use of spoon and fork in south-east Asia is relatively easy, but here there are also precautions. The fork should be held in the left hand and the spoon in the right. However, the fork should not be used to transfer food to the mouth. It should rather be employed to push portions onto the spoon. The American manner of holding the fork in the left hand and shovelling food into the mouth is not considered good manners. The spoon may be used like a knife for cutting up bigger pieces of food.

Evening entertainment

In some Asian countries, fraternisation by males with the opposite sex is more open and accepted than in the West. The entertainment industry therefore caters for this, offering a range of different activities. Occasionally, once a meal is over, further entertainment may be offered, ranging from a drink at another bar, to *Karaoke*, or in the case of male guests, to something more adventurous. The foreign male visitor can fortunately regulate what happens here, by complying with the proceedings as far as he feels comfortable. In many cases the entertainment may be nothing more than the presence of pretty hostesses, who serve drinks and make conversation. This is quite commonplace, and the western guest can blend in quite easily by conversing politely – usually the conversation is nothing more than small talk. Although western women may be invited to such venues as "special guests", such occurrences are rare.

Drinking

In some Asian locations, it is expected that guests should partake of significant quantities of alcohol and get drunk with their Asian counterparts. Relationship-building may be proportional to the amount of alcohol consumed during such sessions! This applies particularly in China, Korea and Japan. In such societies, it is beneficial to know what kind of alcohol will be served and to regulate its rate of consumption. Some local liquors contain in excess of 50% alcohol.

Karaoke

Originating from Japan, *Karaoke* ("empty orchestra") has spread throughout Asia and is now one of the more common forms of entertainment for relationship-building in the East. *Karaoke* venues, also known as *KTV* lounges, abound in most Asian cities. They comprise private, sound-proofed lounges with a bar and snack service. Each lounge is equipped with special audio-visual equipment that plays a TV media clip, while the instrumental backing of a song is played. The words of the song appear as subtitles on the screen and are highlighted as the song progresses, so as to aid the singer. There is a microphone, linked to an audio system, that can be passed around to performers. A tune is selected from a catalogue, and the participant is expected to provide the vocal component of the song by singing through the microphone.

Karaoke bars cater for all groups, be it mixed-gender, all-female or men-only. In the latter case hostesses may also be present. Their job is to sit with guests, serve drinks and enter song selections into the system.

Visiting westerners should expect to participate in *Karaoke* sessions. One way to avoid embarrassment is to compile in advance a repertoire of a few numbers that are easy to sing. *KTV* lounges have expansive lists of common, popular English songs, so the chance of finding one's selection is high.

Going forward

The "generic" guidelines that have been presented in this chapter can be applied to most Asian countries. For better results though, becoming familiar with aspects of etiquette unique to individual countries will be advantageous. To facilitate this process, Part II details specific issues that pertain to the main trading countries of the Far East.

3   Religious and philosophical influences

The primary religions and philosophies of Asia influence cultural values and etiquette in different countries. The dominant influences are:

- Confucianism
- Taoism
- *Theravada* Buddhism
- *Mahayana* Buddhism
- Islam
- Shinto
- Hinduism
- Shamanism

Of these, Confucianism and Taoism, which both originated from China and spread through south-east Asia, are considered the foundation of most Asian behaviour. Superimposed on these founding beliefs are influences of dominant local religions and customs.

In many Asian countries, small but significant groups of followers of Christianity exist. These Asians may be Catholic, Protestant or "free-thinking" Christians. Despite the alignment of their religious followings with those of the West, they do not abandon their deep-rooted Asian beliefs. In most cases they retain their basic Asian identity, and continue to think and act in the Oriental way.

Confucianism

Presence

Confucianism, while having religious aspects, is primarily a set of rules that determine how followers should behave in their daily lives. It is inherently a conservative belief system. Since its inception in China shortly before the birth of Christ, it has become the backbone of Asian behaviour throughout the region. Thus many Asians, regardless of their nationality, have latent Confucian beliefs.

Origins

Confucius lived between 551 and 479 BC. He was born and raised in the state of Lu (now known as Shandong), a province in central east China. Most of his life was spent in government and politics, culminating in his election as prime minister of Lu at the age of 51. Over the years he developed his doctrines, and after terminating his leadership began a crusade across the country promoting his ideals. He finally died aged 73. Subsequently, over the centuries, his tenets experienced several transformations. The most important was that facilitated by Mencius, who assembled Confucian discourses and sayings into books, later known as *Analects*. In 1912, at the end of the last Dynasty, Confucianism was finally classified as an official religion by the Chinese government and Confucius confirmed as a god. Confucian temples of worship were also erected, and are still in use today.

Principles

The *Confucian Analects* contain vast numbers of sayings and philosophies that over time have moulded the attitudes and behaviour of Chinese people. Confucian ways determine proper manners for greetings, behaviour in the company of others, performance at work and most importantly, respect for the aged and parents. The key principles are:

a) Man has five main responsibilities ("laws"):

> To his ruler
> To his father
> To his wife
> To his elder brother
> To his friend

b) The Superior Man

Man should strive to be "superior" for a successful life. Confucius differentiates between a "superior" and an "inferior" man through their behaviour in certain circumstances.

Aspect	Behaviour	
	Superior Man	**Inferior Man**
Demeanour	Quiet and serene	Anxious
Manners	Congenial	Vulgar
Attitude	Dignity without arrogance	Arrogance without dignity
Under stress	Composed	Agitated

It is therefore possible to appreciate Chinese versus westerners' ways when it comes to showing respect for family, seniors and elders, and maintaining composure under duress. By Confucian standards, westerners displaying aggressive and outgoing behaviour are classified as "inferior".

Confucius commented little about the role of women in society, although his opinions have been observed as being somewhat disparaging. For instance, in some Shandong province households where Confucian ways still prevail, the wife, having cooked a family meal, may not always join the men at the table to eat. This exemplifies how Confucian beliefs may have contributed to male dominance in Asian business over the centuries.

Taoism

Presence

Like Confucianism, Taoism (also spelt Daoism) originated in China around the birth of Christ. Over the years there was a degree of conflict between the two beliefs, despite their principles being complementary in certain ways. The influence of Taoism in Asia is not as great and widespread as that of Confucianism, but is also observed mainly by the Chinese.

Origins

Taoism originated from an old philosopher called Lao Tzu. His name means "grand old master", a term of endearment. It is claimed that he was born in China around 604 BC, already aged over 60, as a wise old man with white hair. Apparently his mother, while pregnant with him, was so shocked by the sight of a shooting star that she continued to carry him in her womb for more than 60 years!

Lao Tzu is believed to have worked as an archivist in the Imperial Library, and unlike Confucius was a loner. He did not openly preach his beliefs, yet somehow they became ingrained in Chinese society. He eventually decided to leave China for Tibet, but prior to departing committed his thoughts to writing in a compilation, later known as the *Tao Te Ching* ("The Way and its Power"). This eventually became the bible of Taoist preaching. The *Tao Te Ching* defines the principles of life and endeavours to chart man's existence on earth, espousing harmony within the universe and mankind. This explains why in these modern times, Chinese prioritise harmonious relationship-building in both social and business circles.

Principles

Over the years, Taoism in China was exposed to a number of influences and changes that eventually moulded it into a belief with three divergent variations:

Philosophical: An attitude towards life, probably a continuation of Lao Tzu's original principles.

Religious: Arising from Buddhist influences, leading to the formation of *Tao Chiao* that contains superstitious elements. Texts of religious Taoism state that if certain rituals are performed, miracles may occur. Spirit worship may also be involved.

Indefinable: This form relates to vitalising one's life, and introduces the concept of *Chi* or "flow of energy" by way of meditation, healthy eating and *Tai Chi*, an exercise involving slow, controlled body movements.

While Confucianism is essentially a set of clearly defined rules, Taoism differs in maintaining that nothing about life can be absolutely defined or understood, as such principles are simply too vast and complex. Lao Tzu claimed that if any follower can lay claim to such an achievement, then they do not truly comprehend the philosophies of Taoism!

Buddhism

Presence

Buddhism is practised in many divergent forms throughout most Asian countries. It is the dominant religion in China, Korea, Thailand and Indochina (Vietnam, Laos, Cambodia and Myanmar). It also appears in Japan under the guise of *Zen*, a term used to describe a wide variety of Buddhist and other religious beliefs. To this day, Buddhism in all its forms is the fourth most widely practised religion in the world.

Origins

Buddhism owes its origins to Siddhartha Gautama, who was born in Nepal in the year 560 BC. He was raised in a sheltered environment by aristocratic parents, beneath the summits of the Himalayas. His destiny was determined during his many excursions away from the family mansion, when he was saddened by his observations of mankind's suffering. At the age of 29, he eventually left home to seek salvation in a life of asceticism. He shaved off his hair and beard, donned a simple yellow robe and began carrying a begging bowl. Today, these symbols of Buddhism are still prevalent in most of Thailand and Indochina.

After embarking on a program of meditation, he eventually experienced *The Great Awakening* and attained the status of Buddha. Following this experience, he realised that a being's existence strays from body to body in what is known today as reincarnation. Buddha spent the next 40 years of his life spreading his word, and recruiting disciples to further broaden the teaching of his principles. He eventually died in northern India in 480 BC. Many Buddhist monasteries and temples were built after his death, some of which were constructed around his relics.

Two and a half centuries after his death, a council of Buddhist monks collected Buddha's teachings in a written form called *Tripitaka* ("three baskets"). This also includes a collection of famous Buddhist discourses known as the *Sutras*. In its original form, written in the *Pali* language from India, the *Tripitaka* comprised 80 volumes. The key message of these scripts is to avoid causing harm or suffering to others.

Principles

In the Buddhist faith, unlike other religions such as Christianity, Islam and Hinduism, there is no official joining or confirmation requirement. One may simply commence practising its beliefs without official enrolment.

The foundations of Buddhism are based on Four Noble Truths that portray its underlying theories:

- Suffering exists.
- Craving and clinging to the wrong things (material possessions), causes suffering.
- It is possible to end suffering.
- Ultimate peace and salvation (termination of suffering) can eventually be attained through an eight-fold path.

Thus Buddhism acknowledges that material things (possessions and experiences) do not bring permanent satisfaction. Although short-term gratification is possible through ownership or experience, disappointment or unhappiness will occur later. Man's love for a good life and things associated with it ultimately lead to downfall. Only when man's desires have been removed will he be relieved of suffering. Buddhism advises that this realisation occurs through a process of reincarnation, through which followers eventually become "enlightened", realise self-actualisation and enter a world of *Nirvana*. Thus Buddhists believe they can pass through a number of different lives and upon death reappear in another form, be it another human, animal or being.

Entry into *Nirvana* is the ultimate goal and once this is reached, followers are liberated from further reincarnation. An individual passing through a number of reincarnations is known as a *Bodhisattva* or "Buddha in waiting". During these periods, Buddhists seek relief from suffering by living righteously and practising meditation. Performing good deeds or acts, known as *karma* can accelerate the rate of progress towards *Nirvana*.

There is a perception that every symbol of Buddha on earth has a transcendent counterpart that can be seen in meditation and prayer. Ceremonial giving to such images is practised, as a visit to any temple in Thailand will reveal.

Followers show their respect by offering three burning incense sticks, each representing one of the *Triple Gems* of Buddhism. These are the three elements of the religion that Buddha decreed devotees should respect:

- ◻ The Lord Buddha himself.
- ◻ Buddha's laws – the Dharma.
- ◻ Buddha's community of monks.

In the centuries before and after the birth of Christ, two principal forms of Buddhism emerged in Asia, these being classified into the northern and southern sects. The southern sect found its way into Sri Lanka, Thailand and Indochina, while the northern sect permeated into China, Korea, Japan and Vietnam. The southern form is now termed *Theravada* (or *Hinayana*), while the northern form is known as *Mahayana*. *Mahayana* is considered an extension of *Theravada*, appealing to a broader mass of people. For this reason it is known as "The Greater Vehicle"; correspondingly *Theravada* Buddhism is called "The Lesser Vehicle".

Of the two forms, *Therevada* Buddhism is the more orthodox, closely following the original teachings of the Lord Buddha, as expressed in the Pali script. It practices the belief that final personal salvation (entry into *Nirvana*) of *Bodhisattvas* will only be attained by practising correct behaviour as they pass from life to life. It also advocates time-consuming meditation as part of a monastic lifestyle. Many young men of the *Theravada* sect, before they reach the age of 25, become "temporary monks" just as Gautama did many centuries ago. They shave their heads, wear orange robes and enter a monastic life for three months.

This process is usually timed to coincide with the rainy season so as to expose them to an austere life filled with discipline, religious study, meditation and prayer. While some monks may enter a monastery adjacent to a temple, others take more extreme measures by living in the forest, which facilitates deeper meditation. During their time of priesthood, monks are expected to preach five basic commandments to Buddhist followers:

- Do not kill.
- Do not steal.
- Do not lie.
- Do not commit adultery.
- Do not consume alcohol.

If a monk is over the age of twenty, he is required to follow 227 rules. If he is younger than this, only ten rules have to be obeyed. These are the five listed above, plus the following five:

- Do not touch money.
- Do not use perfume.
- Do not sleep in a comfortable bed.
- Do not sing or dance.
- Do not eat between noon and sunrise.

In adhering to these practices, monks learn to appreciate the futility of a life of luxury and the suffering associated with it. At Buddhist assemblies, followers receive blessings from monks and endeavour to raise their positive *karma,* by not breaking any of the basic commandments for at least the next 24 hours, if not for longer.

Mahayana Buddhism emerged when it was realised that the *Theravada* version permitted *Bodhisattvas* to achieve only personal salvation. *Mahayana* Buddhism is a religion that is freer and more amenable to a wider range of people, and is also considered an expansion of the *Theravada* form. It therefore believes that the religion can change over time and according to circumstance. Examples of this are the many sects of Zen that can be found in Japan.

Mahayana preaches that a *Bodhisattva* should not only strive for personal salvation, but more importantly should seek universal salvation for all mankind. A *Theravada Bodhisattva* believes in ultimately reaching *Nirvana* and transforming into a Buddha, by meditation, worship and ceremonial gift-giving to Buddha. *Mahayana* worshippers follow a different route, by utilising the same noble practices for the salvation of mankind as a whole. The more servility shown to others, through a sense of caring, the greater the degree of personal satisfaction.

Islam

Presence

Muslim beliefs are widely distributed throughout Asia, and have a significant presence in most countries, with the exception of Japan and Korea. Islam is most prevalent in Indonesia and Malaysia, while minority Muslim communities exist in western China, Thailand, the Philippines and Singapore.

Origins

The beginnings of Islam can be traced back to around 572 AD, in Mecca, Saudi Arabia. This was the year of the birth of Mohammed, the prophet who was credited with introducing Islam to the world.

Mohammed was born to a poor family of an Arabic tribe, the *Koreish*. His father died two months before his birth, and his mother died when he was six years old. He was left in the foster care of his uncle. At the age of 25 he began working for Khadija, a wealthy widow, who eventually married him. Being spared the tasks of labour, Mohammed spent many hours in meditation and was able to undertake annual visits, for prayer and meditation, to a mountain named Hira. He returned from one such trip proclaiming to have been chosen as the Prophet of God (*Allah*). This followed a vision (a visit by the Angel Gabriel) that he experienced in a cave at Hira. It is maintained that the Angel Gabriel recited to him what are today the contents of the Islamic holy book, the *Qur'an* ("Koran"). Mohammed was able to remember all that was recited to him, and over a 22-year period he assembled these revelations into verses. Being illiterate, he was unable to compile his words and visions into a unified text, so his brother-in-law and peers helped him to collate these into the *Qur'an*, comprising 114 chapters and 6 236 verses. By the age of 40, Mohammed was actively promoting his new religion. This became a threat to the local tribes and following an assassination attempt in 622, he and a few of his worshippers migrated to Medina. From this new base Mohammed was able to cultivate more followers, and in 630 he was able to conquer Mecca, eventually gaining control of Saudi Arabia. He eventually died in 632. To this day, both Medina and Mecca remain important religious visiting sites for Muslim pilgrims. After the 11th century, Islam spread to south-east Asia through Malaysia and Indonesia, with the arrival of Arab traders from the Middle East.

The formative years of development of Islam in Saudi Arabia resulted in an orthodox form known as *Sunni*, that recognised the *Qur'an* as an eternal, complete and final authority. However, shortly after Mohammed's death, a minority opposition group emerged, proclaiming that their ruling religious leader had the authority of Allah to add to, or alter, the *Qur'an*. This Shi'a (or *Shi'ite*) group is seen today as the more radical of the two sects.

Recently, even more radical sects have emerged, such as Al-Qaeda and Jemiah Islamia, a violent south-east-Asia-based group. Despite this, may other non-violent sects of Islam have evolved, including amalgamations with other religions: for instance the religion of the Indian Sikhs combines both Islamic and Hindu beliefs.

Principles

The literal meaning of Islam is "peace", although it can also be translated as "submission" – surrendering one's own pleasure for the sake of Allah. The *Qur'an* states that Islamic followers have a choice between good and evil, and that Allah's pleasure should be sought through faith, prayer and charity. Muslims strive to maximise their chances of salvation by increasing the proportion of good deeds they perform relative to the number of sins. There is a striking resemblance between the tenets of Islam and Christianity, as evidenced by similarities of verses in the Bible and the *Qur'an*.

Muslims have five principal duties to perform, known as "The Pillars of Islam":

◻ Witnessing the unity of Allah and the Prophet. Declaring that there is no being worthy of worship other than Allah, and that Mohammed is His messenger to all human beings.

◻ Following prescribed daily prayer rituals, five times a day, in accordance with codes set out in the *Qur'an*.

◻ Payment of *Zakat*, a religious tax, as contribution to the social well-being of poorer communities.

◻ Observing the fasting month of *Ramadan*, and the rites that apply during this period.

◻ Undergoing a pilgrimage to Mecca (the *Haj*, or *Umrah*) at least once, provided it is affordable and that one's health permits the journey. A pilgrim, in undertaking the *Haj*, should not impose financial hardship on any fellow pilgrims or their dependants.

The Law of Islam, or *Shari'ah* law, prescribes what is permissible (*halal*) and what is forbidden (*haram*). Everything that is not *haram* as defined by the *Qur'an*, is deemed *halal*. There are some acts deemed *haram*:

◻ Consumption of pork or meat from an animal that has not been slaughtered in accordance with Islamic law.

◻ Consumption of alcohol.

◻ Gambling.

◻ Watching sexually explicit performances.

◻ Dressing in a provocative manner.

◻ Physical contact between unmarried men and women.

The form of Islam practised in the Kingdom of Saudi Arabia is the strictest, where prayer rituals (five a day, and more frequently during *Ramadan*) are rigidly observed. Punishments for theft and adultery entail amputation of a hand or a public beheading. Arab men are permitted to have up to four wives, provided that the husband can afford to keep and maintain them on an equal basis. Men in the Middle East, being extremely wealthy, are able to take advantage of this rule. Most of their poorer counterparts in south-east Asia, namely those in Indonesia and Malaysia, limit themselves to only one wife for economic reasons.

As Islam preaches that Muslims are superior to other believers, it may be difficult for a non-Muslim westerner to establish a good relationship with a Muslim. In the Saudi Arabia women are required to keep their faces and bodies fully covered, and separate public facilities exist for men and women.

Islam purports that processes will occur *Insh'Allah* or "if God is willing". This encompasses the belief that Allah will decide if and when an event should happen. In certain instances, this reason may be given as an excuse for a task or commitment that has not been completed as timeously as expected.

In Islamic countries, all these traits can impinge on the progress of business, particularly during the month of *Ramadan*, when no food or drink is permitted to pass a Muslim's lips between sunrise and sunset. Co-operation levels during this time may be lower, as fasters wrestle with empty stomachs and tired bodies.

In some areas of Asia, Islamic rules are more relaxed and religious sects are less strict. For instance, some Muslims in China are known to eat pork. Sometimes prayers are not said five times a day. But in most countries, at midday on Friday (the most sacred time of the week), Muslim men will visit a mosque to pray.

Hinduism

Presence

Hinduism, with roughly one billion followers, is the third largest religion in the world, behind Christianity and Islam. It is the predominant religion of India and Nepal, and there are large minority Hindu groups in Bangladesh and Sri Lanka.

Hinduism spread to south-east Asia between 800 and 1400 AD, but was rapidly superseded by Buddhism and Islam. A large Hindu population of two million people remains on the Indonesian island of Bali. Both Singapore and Malaysia have significant Hindu minority groups.

Hinduism is limited almost entirely to the Indian culture, as it is not a religion that can be assumed voluntarily. True followers can only be of Hindu parenthood.

Origins

Hinduism is the oldest religion in the world, with its first vestiges dating back earlier than 1500 BC. The precise origins of the religion are not entirely clear, but the traditional view claims that it is an amalgamation of *Vedism* and the "valley culture" of the people of northern India. *Vedism* was introduced by Aryan people from Russia and central Asia when they invaded northern India.

There are several views regarding the derivation of the name Hindu. The most common theory is that it is a Persian corruption of the name of the Indus River, situated in India. Another opinion is that it was formulated from syllables taken from the name of the **Hi**malayan Mountains and the adjacent land of Bi**ndu** Sarovara. Following the initial Vedic period, and after the birth of Christ, many different sects of Hinduism emerged.

A number of sacred texts have also been written, the primary of these being the *Vedas* (derived from the word "Vid" meaning "knowledge") containing hymns, incantations and rituals from ancient India. These were initially formulated in 1500 BC and passed down by word of mouth until they were finally committed to writing in 600 BC. The *Vedas* have no founder and no single source of authority. Another important text is the *Bhagavao Gita*, a collection of God's answers to man's questions about life. In this Hindu bible, the character Krishna represents an incarnation of God.

Principles

Hinduism has no single theological system or central religious organisation. There is no congregational worship. There are many ways that the religion can be categorised, ranging from monotheistic to polytheistic. It can perhaps best be described as a religion that worships both deities and a large number of gods and goddesses. Hindus believe in transmigration of the soul – the transfer of life into another body through many lifetimes (*samsara*). There is no dominant form of Hinduism, although there are four common goals of life (*purusharthas*):

- Dharma: righteousness through correct behaviour.
- Artha: acquisition of wealth.
- Kama: gratification of desire.
- Moksha: liberation from *Samsara* (or emancipation).

Striving for these goals facilitates a self-restrained, balanced and harmonious way of life. Through pure acts and thoughts, a Hindu can be reborn at a higher level. Bad deeds can result in rebirth at a low level, such as an animal or a financially poor human being. Wealth, prestige and suffering are all consequences of one's acts in previous lives.

One of the supreme principles of Hinduism is that of Brahman philosophy, which proclaims a way of life over which three gods preside:

- Brahma: The Creator of new realities.
- Vishnu: The Preserver of creations.
- Shiva: The Destroyer.

Most urban Hindus follow one of two primary forms of the religion:

- Vishnavaism: regards Vishnu as the ultimate deity.
- Shivaism: regards Shiva as the ultimate deity.

Regardless of their sect, Hindus believe in pilgrimages to the ancient city of Benares, situated on the banks of the River Ganges. This is perceived as the most holy city in India.

In the Hindu faith, the cow is considered sacred and for this reason many Indians are vegetarian and specifically do not eat beef and may be averse to leather products. The beast is seen as a provider of milk, and should therefore not be slaughtered.

Shintoism

Presence

The practice of Shinto is unique to Japan and, unlike many religions and philosophies, has not spread to other regions of the world.

Origins

The word Shinto means "way of the gods". It has no clear doctrines or theologies, no historical founder and no single figure of worship, as is found in Christianity, Buddhism and Islam. For many years before the birth of Christ, it existed among agrarian communities in a non-defined form, without structure or name. It was only officially given a name following the arrival of Buddhism in the 6th century. For many centuries Buddhism and Shinto co-existed, often sharing the same places of religious worship. Up until the Meiji Restoration period that began in 1868, Shinto was subservient to Buddhism with many Shinto shrines being located within the grounds of Buddhist Temples. Whereas Buddhist Temples are defined by their relatively large structures, Shinto shrines (*Jinja*) are identified by a gateway (*Torii*) of two slanting upright supports bearing cross pieces. *Torii* are usually noticeable by their vermillion colour.

After his enthronement in 1868, the Japanese Emperor Meiji realised the need to strengthen the Japanese identity and decreed Shinto as the state religion. Shinto shrines were granted higher status, and the religion advanced at the expense of Buddhism. Many Buddhist temples and images were destroyed, while others were incorporated into Shinto shrines. Shinto was sponsored by the state and any opposition was promptly crushed. During the Second World War, Shinto contributed to Japan's expansionist military objectives, by promoting aggressive invasion of other Asian countries. It was only after the defeat of Japan in 1945 that new policies were implemented, granting freedom of religious belief including the cessation of state sponsorship of any religion.

Principles

Prior to the arrival of Buddhism in Japan, Shinto was nothing more than a poorly defined religion aligned with nature and believing in deities, or *kami*. Deities are mythological creatures perceived to have influential powers. They can be ancestors, departed beings, the spirits of past emperors, living creatures or even inanimate objects. Emperor Meji was deemed to be a *kami* during his period of rule. As the economy in early Japan was mostly agrarian, homage was paid to those *kami* that could influence the outcome of favourable crop harvests. One old and important *kami* was named *Inari*, god of the rice harvest. In modern times he is now also worshipped as the god of business.

Today, Shinto believers focus on acquiring blessings, particularly for children, during critical moments of their lives. Shinto worship primarily relates to influencing events that pertain to life on earth, and avoids issues relating to death or the after-life. This is contrary to Buddhism, which deals with the realities of death and subsequent reincarnations. Following tradition, many Japanese have ingrained Shinto beliefs in one form or another.

Shamanism

Presence

Shamanism, otherwise known as belief in the spirit world, exists throughout Asia as an ethereal form of worship, with unique sets of norms and values. It is considered the "default" religion of south-east Asia, and extends down from China.

Origins

Owing to the many and varied forms of spirit worship, no single origin of Shamanism can be traced. However, there is evidence to suggest that one source is Taoism, in which a spirit "Jade Emperor" was worshipped. Spirits may also be historical heroes, may of whom are women.

Principles

There are usually three types of spirit cult:

- ☐ Village guardians who protect communities.
- ☐ Departed heroes.
- ☐ Ancestral spirits.

In many cases living mediums (mostly women) are used to communicate with spirits of the dead. Owing to the varied, secretive and mysterious ways in which Shamanism is practised, westerners often find it difficult to comprehend the ways of spirit believers. Although considered a minority religion, Shamanism is often practised with other primary religions. For instance, Chinese Buddhists worship the spirits of their dead relatives. Buddhists in Thailand and Indochina turn to mediums to communicate with spirit-like gods for help in times of trouble, or when crucial decisions have to be made. Important business decisions may therefore be based on the opinions of the spirits. For example, new investment projects may not proceed until the spirits feel that the time is right.

PART 2

Etiquette in selected Asian countries

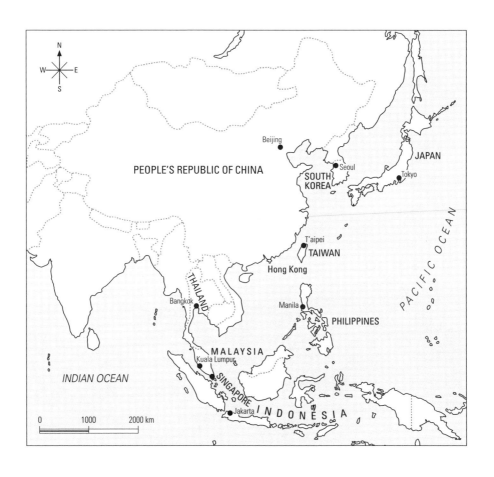

4   Greater China

The three Chinese regions, the People's Republic of China (PRC) or "China", the Special Administrative Region (SAR) of Hong Kong, and Taiwan, also known as the Republic of China (ROC), are referred to as "Greater China". China is by far the largest and most significant of the three Chinese territories. The origins of Hong Kong and Taiwan are inextricably linked with those of China, with the result that all display similar Chinese traits. There are, however minor variances between these three regions, particularly in their attitude to concluding business deals. Of the three, China is the most challenging for westerners, owing to the higher levels of bureaucracy, and the greater degree of interference of both government and regional authorities in private business.

With world globalisation as it is today, western values are infiltrating China such that younger generations are tending to adopt western ways. A visit to any of the eastern seaboard cities of China, Hong Kong and Taiwan will reveal an emerging sect that is materialistic and less oriented towards traditional Chinese customs. While in some ways this is rather a sad development, it should make bridging the intercultural gap easier in the future. Despite this, westerners still need to be sensitised to Chinese etiquette, particularly when dealing with middle-aged and older people.

People's Republic of China (PRC)

Geographically, China is the third largest country in the world, behind Russia and Canada. It has one of the oldest civilisations known to man, going back over 4 000 years.

Today, it is one of the most exciting growth regions of the world, and is becoming the global focal point for both manufacturing and bilateral trade. East–West interaction in China is on the increase as western companies turn their attention to investment in this country, given that it provides an inexpensive source of labour and a large emerging market. This trend is also impacting on other countries in south-east Asia, as multinational companies relocate their manufacturing operations away from these more expensive regions to China. The recent entry of China into the World Trade Organisation has added a further stimulus to Sino-western relations.

Country background

Population

The population of China exceeds 1.3 billion people. While this presents an enormous opportunity for growth, much of this population is of low economic activity, particularly in the central and western provinces. Reported population growth rates are currently between 1 and 2%, down from the 7% levels of the 1970s. In order to curb the high population growth rate, a "one child per family" policy was introduced during 1980.

Ethnicity and religion

More than 90% of the population are *Han Ren*, or "people of the *Han*", with origins dating back to the *Han* dynasty before the birth of Christ. There are more than 60 other cultures, including Mongols and Tibetans.

China's religious beliefs are a fusion of the influences of Buddhism, Taoism and Confucianism. Because of this, no precise data is available on the percentage composition of each religion. Islam also exists (2 to 3% of the population), particularly in the western province of Xinjiang, around Urumqi. It is also sparsely distributed among the eastern provinces.

Language and script

There are over 100 languages and dialects in China. The main official language is Mandarin, spoken in the central and northern regions. Cantonese is spoken mainly in the south, particularly in the Guangdong province and Hong Kong. *Putonghua* was also devised by the government to be a *lingua franca* for China, and is essentially based on Mandarin. An interesting feature of Chinese writing is that being pictorial, it is universal and conveys the same meaning for each dialect, even though the sound of the same written word may differ between dialects.

It is said that to be proficient in Chinese over 10 000 Chinese characters must be known, and for a basic understanding a minimum of 3 000 is required. Mandarin is a tonal language, such that depending upon its pronunciation a word can have up to four different meanings. Learning Mandarin is therefore a formidable task for any westerner. To assist in this process, a system known as *Hanyu pin yin* ("spelling") was devised, where the phonetic sounds of Chinese words are converted into a Romanised form that can be pronounced by foreigners.

When the Chinese translate numbers verbally into English numeric values, the western recipient of such data should exercise caution and double-check the figure. Owing to the way in which numbers are expressed in Chinese (very large numbers are expressed as multiples of 10 000), there is a possibility that during translation a number may be misquoted by a factor of 10 or more. It is often a good idea to ask that the number be written down in order to eliminate any ambiguity.

Regional structures

China comprises 22 provinces, five autonomous regions and four municipalities (Beijing, Shanghai, Chongqing and Tianjin). It also includes the Special Administrative Regions of Hong Kong and Macau. Hong Kong was formerly a British colony that was ceded back to China in 1997, while Macau was previously a Portuguese colony that was returned in 1999.

Political environment

It is well known that the Government of China is communist. There is a single legislative house, being the National People's Congress, with all 3 500 participants being members of the Communist Party. The members of the National People's Congress are elected every five years by the provinces, special administrative regions and the military. From these members, a state council is elected that is responsible for enactment of legislation. The state president is chief of the state council, and a premier heads the government.

Religious, cultural and historical influences

By tracing the origins of Taoism, Confucianism and Buddhism through to present times, it is possible to appreciate how these have influenced the way Chinese think and behave in their daily lives – a society with distinct attitudes towards harmonious relations between all beings. Their beliefs and customs are far more complex than those of the West, making dealing with the Chinese especially challenging.

Taoism and Confucianism

Taoism and Confucianism form the backbone of Chinese culture around the world. Two famous philosophers, Lao Tzu and Confucius, introduced them into China shortly before the birth of Christ. These beliefs are more philosophical than religious, and both preach harmony and balance in life.

Taoism focuses on the need to maintain harmony between all beings. Confucianism, the more dominant of the two, has been ingrained into the basic way of life of Chinese people across the world. It has clear and specific rules laid out in the *Analects*, the Confucian equivalent of the Bible. One facet of Confucianism is the concept of a "Superior Man", who does not display emotions and maintains a calm demeanour under duress.

Buddhism

Following Taoism and Confucianism, Buddhism is the next largest religion in China. Of the three religions, Buddhism is the only one that preaches reincarnation and the afterlife. Those who practise Buddhism believe that it is only after experiencing a number of cycles of reincarnation, via different living beings, that all the misdeeds and sorrow of life on earth will disappear.

While Buddhism originated in Nepal around 500 BC, it only emerged in China during the 1st century AD, following the migration of monks from India and Nepal.

In its *Mahayana* form (see Chapter 3 for more detail), it spread throughout China, and began competing with Taoism. In order to compete with Buddhism, Taoists introduced their own gods and deities that can be seen in Taoist temples today.

After the collapse of the *Han* dynasty in 220 AD, and until 600 AD, Buddhism gained a foothold over Confucianism and Taoism, so that by the end of this period it had become a new principle order, with many monasteries appearing throughout the country. Buddhism continued its ascent until the 10th century when the ruling emperor of China (Wu-Tsung), dissatisfied with the extent of its spread, ordered the destruction of Buddhist establishments. While this did not completely destroy the religion, it did create an opportunity for Confucianism to dominate again. By the 20th century Buddhism had started a decline, and was dealt a further blow by the arrival of communist rule. During The Cultural Revolution period, open worship was prohibited and all Buddhist monasteries were dismantled. Despite these setbacks, at the end of The Cultural Revolution, Buddhism subsequently staged a comeback and is again widely and openly practised in China today.

Historical Influences

China has one of the oldest civilizations in the world. Records show that the Dynasty period of Chinese Emperors began in 2100 BC.

Britain's involvement with China began in the early 19th century when trade began with the Far East British India Company. However this soured when China prohibited the import of opium from India by the British, culminating in the Opium Wars between 1839 and 1852. These lead to the cession of Hong Kong to England under a 99-year lease.

The Chinese Dynasty system ended in 1912, when it was superseded by democratic rule under the Nationalist Party (Kuomintang) of Dr Sun Yatsen. During the Second World War, China was occupied by Japan. Many atrocities were committed, such as the Rape of Nanking, with the result that China still harbours a latent resentment of Japan.

Following the Allied defeat of Japan, civil war broke out between the Nationalist Party and the communists. The communists were eventually victorious, forcing the Nationalists to retreat to Taiwan in 1949.

Under the leadership of Mao Zedong, the communist People's Republic of China was established. In 1958 he initiated "The Great Leap Forward" by mobilising communal villages into small backyard industries. It was a complete failure. In 1966 he attempted to recover his credibility by initiating "The Cultural Revolution" – a ban on old ideals, customs and habits. All religious beliefs were suppressed. During this time economic development stagnated. It was only after the death of Mao Zedong in 1976 that his successor, Deng Xiaopeng, was able to steer China towards more capitalistic ways.

Mao Zedong is still seen as the father figure of modern China, despite the failure of his initiatives. However, one of Mao's real accomplishments was that he was able to unify what had previously been a fragmented country, and establish a shared vision throughout the nation, albeit under strict communist rule.

Social and business values

The evolution of Taoism, Confucianism and Buddhism in China over the centuries has created a superstitious culture with highly complex and varied attitudes towards life. In line with Confucian principles, the Chinese have a greater respect for seniority and the elderly, and also maintain close-knit family groups. Family values are extremely high, with children remaining in the parental residence until they are married. Offspring have a greater obligation to care for ageing parents.

Although Confucian-dominated countries do not support the emancipation of women in business, unlike Japan and Korea, women do occupy positions of power in China, owing to the influence of communism that preaches "everyone is equal".

Chinese are by nature a polite, but secretive and untrusting culture. They regard anyone outside their inner circle of trust with suspicion. The family unit automatically falls within this circle, while outsiders are only admitted after an acceptable relationship has been established. Even within their own culture, the Chinese are slow to accept others. Those originating from the same village, or speaking the same dialect, are more readily accepted. As foreigners are classified outside the trust circle, extra time and effort should be taken towards relationship-building. The Chinese call white Caucasians *Gwei Lo* (male) and *Gwei Po* (female), derogatory Cantonese terms interpreted as "white spirit" or "white ghost", which refers to their light hair and skin colour. These names also imply that Caucasians are not to be trusted. Locals of China, along with many other populations of developing countries in south-east Asia, believe that Caucasian westerners are very wealthy and therefore charge them over-inflated prices in shops and stores. There is usually a two-tier system of pricing – the "local price" and a much higher "foreign price". To some extent this line of thinking also prevails in business.

In business encounters, a Chinese person evaluates whether or not he will feel comfortable doing business with someone, rather than the organisation that the person represents. Time will have to be spent developing and nurturing an interpersonal relationship in order to establish trust (*xinyong*). Western businessmen often underestimate the importance of this process. When dealing with Chinese entities, it is essential that senior executives take time and effort to accommodate their Chinese counterparts and to ensure that their junior managers do likewise. Chinese protocol requires that at meetings "like should be matched with like" across the chain of seniority. Western companies should consider the implications of frequently rotating staff through their China offices, as new relationships with customers and clients will have to be established, a time-consuming process.

A significant feature of relationships in Chinese life is *guanxi*. Although this manifests itself in a number of ways, it is nothing more than a form of "if you scratch my back, I'll scratch yours". It is practised within circles of trust, where one person will help another to overcome a difficulty. This is usually done with a tacit understanding that a return favour is expected at some future point in time (*renqing*). *Guanxi* affects the way problems are resolved all over Asia. While in business a westerner might focus on directly influencing a key decision-maker, the *guanxi* route uses a more discreet approach, where personal relationships are leveraged with someone else who has more influence over the decision-maker. In dealing with customers, unusual requests that may seem irrelevant or superfluous may be received. Provided they can be acceded to within the limits of acceptable ethics and governance, the extra effort taken can reap handsome rewards over time as a result of the "debt" so created.

Perhaps the most important aspect of interacting with the Chinese (as with all other Asian cultures) in everyday situations, is the need to save (and give) face (*mianzi*). While this is to some degree prevalent in the West, in the Chinese environment it is a far more subtle and complex process. Actions that in the West may appear quite innocent and harmless might well cause loss of face to the Chinese. For instance, even a polite refusal to eat a special Chinese delicacy offered during a meal will cause severe loss of face to the host. Opportunities also exist to give face. Simple examples of this are:

- Complimenting someone on a minor achievement.
- Making concessions during negotiations.

Contrary to western ways, the importance of team performance overrides recognition of individual performance and achievement. Group decision-making is preferred over individual autonomy. The Chinese style of group decision-making, where issues are debated through bureaucratic hierarchies, also creates complicated and longer decision-making processes.

Local customs and etiquette

Special beliefs

Western visitors to China should be aware of the following special beliefs:

- The number "four" is considered unlucky, as it is associated with death (the Mandarin pronunciation of "four" and "death" are nearly identical). Some Chinese will not take a flight or get married on the fourth of the month.
- The number "eight" or any combination of eight (such as 8888) is considered lucky, as in Chinese "eight" sounds like the word "prosperity". It is beneficial to quote prices that include the digit eight.
- The numbers "three" ("life") and "nine" ("eternity") are also considered auspicious.
- The colours red (prosperity) and yellow (gold, wealth) are good colours. Green is also acceptable, signifying longevity. Dark purple, white and black are not acceptable colours.
- Elements of nature, including creatures, have significant meaning:
  - Flowing water implies that money will flow into a business, which is why many Chinese businesses have a water feature at their entrance.
  - A dragon implies great strength and power.
  - Tortoises symbolise long life.
  - Fish are a sign of prosperity, which is why Chinese often have fish tanks either at home or in the office. A gift depicting a fish will be well received.
  - A pair of lions may often be seen guarding the door of a Chinese enterprise – this is to keep evil spirits at bay.

Etiquette

When interacting with Chinese people, **don't**:

- Bite your fingernails in public.
- Beckon with your index finger.
- Write crosses next to people's names or their pictures; a cross or the letter "X" has connotations with death.
- Write a person's name in red ink; this signifies that they are due to die.
- Wink at a person.
- Initiate talk about religions, particularly those considered extremist by the communist government, such as *Falung Gong*. Discussions about Taiwan and Japan should be avoided, as these are also sensitive issues.
- Refer to the PRC as "The Republic of China". This name, specifically reserved for Taiwan, is frowned upon.
- Show irritation at pushing and shoving in shops, buses and trains – such acts are *not* considered impolite.
- Present items such as name cards, gifts, cash notes and credit cards using only one hand; this should rather be done with both hands.
- Take offence at excessive curiosity about your personal background, and being studied closely in public.

Preparation and awareness

Appointment scheduling

Where first-time contact is being established with a Chinese firm, a reply to a written request for a meeting may not be forthcoming. It is preferable to initiate contact using a suitable personal channel of introduction, rather than by sending an impersonal letter. This can be accomplished by using the trade office attached to your home country embassy located in China, or a suitably appointed agent.

The Chinese Lunar New Year period is not a good time to visit China, as most businesses and operations close for at least a week (or two) over this period. Week-long breaks are also taken around Labour Day (1 May) and National Day (first week of October), also known as Golden Week.

When visiting parts of China to the north of Beijing, the winter months of December to March should be avoided, as it is bitterly cold over this period. Heavy snowfalls can occur, preventing airport activities for days at a time and resulting in lengthy delays.

It is appropriate to arrive on time for meetings, as it is possible that the Chinese party may arrive early. As the economy of China continues to burgeon, traffic jams in some of the major cities (especially Beijing, Shanghai, Nanjing and Guangzhou) are becoming more severe. Plenty of time should therefore be allocated for travelling between appointments.

Gifts

Gifts should be wrapped in brightly coloured red or yellow paper. It is considered impolite to present an unwrapped gift. If red paper is used, the colour should not be too dominant. Dark purple and white should be avoided (Taoism associates these with funerals). The following items should be strictly avoided:

◻ Clocks (in Chinese the pronunciation of the word for clock, *zhong* is similar to the phrase "to send someone to their maker" and signifies that death is near). Although watches may be given, to be absolutely safe these should also be avoided.

◻ Knives, scissors or letter-openers (represents a cut in the relationship).

◻ Socks, sandals, handkerchiefs and towels (associated with funerals and grieving).

◻ Flowers, unless they are for the sick, for weddings or for funerals. An even number of flowers should be given. White flowers should not be given as a gift.

◻ Any gift containing a cluster of four items. Four is an unlucky number.

◻ A green hat or cap when presented to a man – this rather strange belief stems from the fact that it signifies that the wearer's wife is having an affair with another man.

An acceptable gift for an important person is a bottle of expensive brandy or red wine, as these are popular beverages in China.

Gifts are given at the conclusion of meetings, and should be passed over to recipients using both hands. The receiver should accept the gift with both hands, together with a slight bow. If a single gift is being given to a group, this should be presented to the most senior person. Sometimes a gift may be refused – it is customary and considered good manners for a recipient to refuse to accept a gift at least three times. The giver should in a humble and polite manner repeatedly request the receiver to accept "this small token of appreciation", until the gift is eventually accepted. It is customary and polite not to open gifts in the presence of the giver.

Dress code

When choosing a wardrobe for business travels in China, it is preferable to select clothing that is conservative in style and colour: for men, a suit and a tie, and for women, conservative suits of neutral colours, with low-heeled shoes.

Name cards

Plenty of name cards (*ming pian*) should be available, as the Chinese are known for bringing large delegations to meetings. If possible, name cards should be printed on both sides, with English on the one side and Chinese on the other.

As a Chinese given name usually describes a positive feature of its owner, westerners should use Chinese characters that portray a flattering meaning, while still resembling the correct pronunciation. As such a translation is quite a delicate process, a knowledgeable Chinese person should be engaged to assist with the design.

Meeting formalities

Names and forms of address

An understanding of the derivation of Chinese personal names, and how they are used, is essential. As described earlier, the English translation of Chinese words is performed by way of a phonetic conversion of the Chinese characters into English words – the *Hanyu pin yin* system.

Many *Hanyu pin yin* words use combinations of letters that are difficult to pronounce. Some of the more common combinations of letters and their pronunciations are given below:

X is a hybrid of "s" as a sibilant and "sh"

e.g. Xu Xin Gong, a man's name, is pronounced "Shu Shin Gong", with a slight sibilant sound to the "sh".

ZH is "ch"

e.g. the city Hangzhou is pronounced "Hungchow".

AN is "un"

e.g. the family name Zhang is pronounced "Chung" and not "Chang".

QI is "chi"

e.g. the city Qingdao is pronounced "Chingdaow".

AO is "aow"

e.g. the man's given name Hao is pronounced as a drawn out "Haow".

CAI is "chye"

e.g. the family name Cai is pronounced "Chye".

A Chinese name normally comprises two or three words. Unlike western names where the surname appears at the end, in Chinese the surname or family name comes first. The remaining word(s) are first or given names. In the case of a male, the first given name (i.e. the middle name) can be passed down through generations. The person Zhu Xia Ming is formally addressed as "Mr Zhu", or informally as "Xia Ming". Sometimes given names are combined, such that they appear as a single word. For instance, using the above name as an example, Mr Zhu's given names could also appear as "Xiaming". Younger Chinese who interact with foreigners in business may substitute their Chinese given name with a western one. For instance, Deng Xiaoyu might change his name to "Jack Deng".

In marriage, a Chinese wife retains her maiden name, while offspring assume their father's family name. It is customary to call a man "Mr", and a woman "Ms" or "Madam". "Mrs" or "Miss" is not normally used. Even after a good relationship has been developed it is preferable to retain the more formal mode of address, using only family names.

Meeting and greeting

During greeting and introduction formalities, care should be taken to shake hands with every person in the delegation. A light grip should be applied and held for a short while. A slight bow or nod of the head while doing this is appropriate. When shaking hands among a group of people, the handshake of one pair should not cut across that of another. This creates a "cross" that symbolises death.

It is not always recommended that a western man shake hands with a Chinese woman. However, provided this is performed briefly and with a light grip, no offence should be caused. A western woman will have to initiate a handshake with a Chinese man.

Business cards should be exchanged using a two-handed technique, whereby the card is handed over by grasping the top two corners with the thumb and index finger of each hand. The card should be presented with the side showing the Chinese version (if applicable), the right way round, so that the receiver can read it as they accept the card.

Preliminaries

Upon arrival at a meeting, the most senior member of a western delegation should enter the room first. The same protocol will apply to the senior member of a Chinese group. However, if he/she has a poor command of English, they may not necessarily lead the discussions. This will be delegated to a subordinate with better English skills. Some Chinese companies employ a person with good English capabilities as a "foreign relations manager" whose job it is to act as liaison with foreign visitors. They are only used to facilitate communications and will not be a key decision maker within the organisation.

On being seated, visiting guests should take the position of honour, being the seats at the back of the room facing the door. The most senior member of a delegation should take the seat located centrally on his or her side of the table.

Negotiation etiquette

It is expected that the most senior member of each team leads the negotiations. On no account should subordinates contradict or interrupt senior members while discussions are in progress. Loud, flamboyant and aggressive presentations should be toned down – a show of humility is considered a virtue among the Chinese. They also believe that it is better to listen than talk, and periods of silence, while unsettling for westerners, are used by Chinese for thinking and reflection. If a Chinese negotiator does not know the answer to a question or disagrees on some issue, a vague answer may be given in order to save face. In most cases, an important request will not be agreed to immediately as the Chinese bureaucratic system usually requires that the matter be referred to more senior groups in the organisation. This can take a considerable period of time, to the point that deadlines may not be met.

Meals and entertainment

Invitations

On occasions, during business trips to China, invitations to meals will be received. It is recommended that such invitations be accepted, as this is an opportunity for relationship-building. Should it not be possible to accept an invitation, an alternate time should be suggested. Dinner is normally considered the main form of entertainment in the Chinese environment, and in the business world can sometimes be quite a formal affair.

Chinese are generally not broad-minded when it comes to tasting foreign cuisine. When hosting them for a meal, be it in China or at home, it is preferable to take them to a fine Chinese restaurant rather than a western facility.

Food and drink

It is said that the Chinese will eat anything that has legs and has its back pointing towards the sky, except a table! This is generally true, even to the extent that "edible" creatures don't necessarily have to have legs, meaning that snakes and worms can also be included as part of the menu! It is possible that you may encounter dishes containing dog, cat, monkey and various insects. Roast scorpion is one such example. If westernised Chinese people are acting as hosts, they may "protect" foreigners by ordering "safe" dishes that are more acceptable to the western palate. No matter what is served, an effort should be made to sample the fare regardless of how unappetising it may appear, and on no account should distaste be shown via facial expression. It would cause the host loss of face if such food were to be refused, as it may have been ordered as a special delicacy in the guest's honour.

The type of dish served may vary from province to province. The central province of Sizhuan is renowned for its extremely spicy food, while in the southern province of Guangdong Cantonese cooking prevails – this cuisine tends to be less spicy and slightly sweet.

In a Chinese menu the main dish is usually fish, which is served as one of the last courses. This is normally steamed, served whole and placed in the centre of the table. The Chinese believe that food should be as fresh as possible when served. Ideally, fish should be cooked immediately after being caught, which is why tanks containing live fish can be seen outside some restaurants. In some cases, diners are allowed to select their choice from a fish tank immediately before its preparation for the table.

The Chinese believe that drinking is an excellent way of dispensing with barriers, so when the opportunity arises this activity should be welcomed. Travelling northwards through China, the pastime of drinking becomes more prevalent because of the extreme cold in winter, and the need to keep warm. When Chinese hosts ask guests "do you drink?" they are inquiring if they can tolerate large quantities of alcohol, without getting drunk. Caution should therefore be exercised in responding to this question. "Non-drinkers" can use the excuse that they are taking medication that reacts unfavourably with alcohol, or that their religion prohibits it. Those visitors having a weak constitution should carefully pace their rate of alcohol consumption during such drinking sessions.

Alcoholic drinks vary from beer (*pijiu*), local Chinese wine (*huangjiu*), foreign red wine (*hongjiu*), to a potent local liquor called *baijiu*. *Baijiu* is distilled from fermented rice, wheat and sorghum and contains in excess of 50% alcohol. A popular brand and generic name is *Maotai*, which contains over 55% alcohol. It is consumed out of a small liqueur glass and should be imbibed with extreme caution. *Huangjiu* ("yellow wine" – but more brown in colour) is usually served at the beginning of a meal. It has a lower alcohol content than *baijiu* and tastes like diluted sherry. It is not uncommon for *huangjiu* and *baijiu* to be served simultaneously. Red, rather than white wine is usually served, as the Chinese believe its colour will bring prosperity, as well as being good medicine for the heart.

Table etiquette

The Chinese meal is taken seated around a large circular table, with the most senior host and guest seated at the far side of the table, facing the entrance to the room. The most senior member of the guest delegation is seated to the right of the most senior host, with the next most senior guest seated on his left. The next most senior host is positioned at the opposite side of the table, with less senior guests seated either side of him. Should an interpreter be present, they will be seated to the right of the senior guest. To facilitate the allocation process, guests should allow the senior host to allocate their seats at the table.

The place setting usually comprises a bowl for soup, rice or noodles, and a small plate on which to place selected food items. Chopsticks and a flat-based spoon are provided. Although restaurants in major centres will provide western-style eating utensils, this might not be the case in rural areas. It will cause loss of face to those who have to resort to a using a knife and fork in a Chinese restaurant, so be prepared to manage with chopsticks at all times! If you experience difficulty managing a morsel with chopsticks, it is permissible to pick up the flat spoon with the left hand (for right-handed people), push it into the spoon using chopsticks in the right hand, and eat from the spoon. Details of chopstick etiquette, as given in Chapter 2, should be studied as a precursor to visiting any Chinese region.

Chinese green tea is always poured throughout the meal, being served without milk or sugar. This is deemed to be healthy, as an aid to digestion. In less formal eating establishments, particularly in rural areas, local diners use tea served at the table to wash their hands, soup bowl and eating plate before the meal commences.

The host normally selects the menu, and it is considered impolite for a guest to intervene and order a dish. In China, dishes are shared and not served as individual orders, as done in the western environment. A large number of dishes are placed in the centre of the table from which diners may help themselves. Small portions are selected from the main dish, either with chopsticks or a serving spoon, and placed on individual eating plates. Pieces selected from the main dish should first be placed on the eating plate and not transferred directly to the mouth.

At the beginning of the meal, a number of cold meat or vegetarian dishes may appear, followed by soup, and then a series of hot dishes, finishing with rice or noodles. Soup is taken throughout the meal and is consumed using the flat-bottomed spoon. It is not polite to pick up the soup bowl and drink from it, as is done in Japan. Morsels of food in the soup may be picked out and eaten with chopsticks or the flat-bottomed spoon.

Fish, when served whole, is divided up into pieces at the table. The fish may be placed on the table with its head facing the guest of honour, and should not be moved from this position. It is considered bad luck to turn the fish over to access the meat underneath. In the sailing or fishing environment, this is tantamount to signifying that a boat will capsize or sink. The tastiest part of the fish is the head – the eye is considered the real delicacy. The head is reserved for the most important guest, and may by served by the host as a sign of honour. The honoured guest is expected to partake of the flesh (the cheek) from the fish head. When chicken is served, the head of the chicken may also appear on the main serving dish. In this case, it is intended only for decoration purposes and should not be presented to anyone, as it will bring bad luck to the recipient.

Rice or noodles are normally served near the end of the meal, just prior to dessert. These are considered "fillers" in case diners have not had enough to eat during the main meal. Steamed or fried rice is served into a bowl. It is permissible to pick up the bowl and place it close to the mouth, transferring the rice with the chopsticks. Noodles can be taken "wet" or "dry". Dry noodles usually appear in fried form, without much liquid. Alternatively they can be taken "wet", in soup form, along with other ingredients.

Dessert is either cut fresh fruit, a vegetable dish such as red bean soup, mango pudding or sago pudding. Chinese desserts are usually quite acceptable to the western palate.

Table etiquette dictates that:

- Business should not be discussed during the meal. Such time should be used to nurture the relationship, by asking about family life etc.
- Guests should allow the host to begin eating first, or for the host to invite them to begin eating.
- It is possible that the host will select some special morsel from the table and place it on a guest's plate; this is a sign of respect, for which thanks should be given. The morsel should be eaten.
- Morsels of food should not be selected from the main serving dish by "picking and hunting" with chopsticks. The piece to be selected should be visually identified first before it is taken from the dish.
- Food should not be piled up on the eating plate from the main serving dish.
- It is permissible from a seated position to stretch across the table to select food from a dish; however, it is considered impolite to stand and reach across the table.
- When reaching across to select something from the table, one's arm or chopsticks should not cross that of another person as this creates an "X", a sign of death.
- Dishes should be handed around the table, and not passed across the table.
- Morsels such as chicken bones and shrimps in the shell should not be eaten with the fingers. These should be handled with chopsticks only. Bones and crustacean shells should be removed from the mouth with chopsticks and placed on a side plate, or in the absence of a plate, placed directly on the table.

◘ Once a bite has been taken out of a selected piece of food, it should not be dipped back into a communally shared sauce.

◘ At the end of the meal, a small amount of food should be left on the plate otherwise the host will continue to offer more food. Leaving a clean plate implies that not enough food was served, causing loss of face to the host.

◘ At large formal dinners, it is advisable to drink alcohol only when toasts are called for (of which there could be many!).

◘ The mouth should be covered with the hand while using toothpicks to remove food particles from the teeth.

◘ If there is a need to smoke, cigarettes should first be offered to other diners.

During meals and drinking sessions, the host may call on a particular guest to *ganbei*, the Mandarin equivalent of "bottoms up", meaning "dry glass". The nominated person is expected to drain their glass along with the host. Thereafter, the process may be repeated many times throughout the meal among those present. It is considered appropriate for the senior guest to offer a reciprocal toast to the principle host. To avoid an over indulgence of alcohol, drinking glasses should be kept as empty as possible and only drunk from when called upon to *ganbei*. Drinking stamina is gauged on how well the higher alcohol content beverages are tolerated. Where possible, an effort should be made to keep pace with the others, thereby demonstrating a strong constitution. This will generate a degree of admiration and respect. During drinking sessions, a favourable impression can be created by complimenting a Chinese person on being a "strong drinker".

To show appreciation to a Chinese host for his hospitality, a gift may be presented at the end of the meal. This should not, however, be a food item, as this will imply that the meal was insufficient. The best way to reciprocate is to issue an invitation for another meal at a later date.

Evening entertainment

Once a meal is over, diners do not normally linger at the table and the party will usually break up to go home or to move on to some other entertainment. Occasionally, further drinking sessions at another venue, such as a *Karaoke* bar, may be suggested. In the main commercial city of Shanghai, many restaurant chains are to be found in Hengshan Road, while the new area of Xintindi is a popular place to gather for after-dinner drinks. Xintindi is an historic part of the city that has been modernised, and has a number of live music bars where plenty of action can be found.

Special Administrative Region of Hong Kong (SAR)

The Special Administrative Region (SAR) of Hong Kong (or *Xiang Gang* in Mandarin) comprises a small southern portion of mainland China, Kowloon (or *Gow Lung*, meaning "nine dragons") and the New Territories, as well as an island (Hong Kong), which is a five-minute ferry ride from the mainland.

There are 234 smaller islands, many of which are uninhabited and mountainous. Most commercial and financial activities are located on Hong Kong, while manufacturing is undertaken in the New Territories.

The SAR came into being in 1997, when the region was returned to China upon termination of a 99-year lease held by the British. Prior to this it was a British colony, having a large expatriate population exerting considerable western influence.

For a period of fifty years following the 1997 handover, the legal, social and economic systems of this former UK colony are to be retained under a "one country two system" basis. It was, and still is, a stepping stone for foreign business into China. Despite being designated a "special region" with more democracy than China itself, this is slowly changing. Ultimately, Hong Kong will lose the vestiges of its former colonial ways and be homogenised with the rest of the China.

Country background

Population

The population of Hong Kong is seven million people, and continues to expand rapidly. As freedom of movement from China into Hong Kong is increasing, there is a large influx of both legal and illegal immigrants from China.

Ethnicity and religion

Over 95% of the population are Chinese, and less than 2% are European. Of the Chinese, most come from the southern provinces of China, such as Guangdong, located on the northern borders of the New Territories.

There is no official religion in Hong Kong. Most of the populace follows the Chinese beliefs of Confucianism, Taoism and Buddhism. It is estimated that at least 10% of the population is Christian.

Language and script

Hong Kong has two official languages – English and Chinese. The main Chinese dialect is Cantonese, unique to the southern provinces of China. Cantonese is often spoken loudly, and is tonal, like Mandarin. Whereas Mandarin has four tones, Cantonese has at least eight. Many Hong Kong Chinese do not understand Mandarin. This is changing as more schools in Hong Kong are teaching students Mandarin. Hong Kong uses the older more traditional written Chinese characters which differ from the newer, simplified version used in China. Classic Chinese text is read downwards in columns, from right to left across a page, such that books and magazines appear to be read from back to front.

Regional structures

Hong Kong is ruled as one administrative region. In an effort to empower inhabitants, 18 district boards have been established, comprising government officials and other elected local representatives.

Political environment

Prior to the return of Hong Kong to China, a governor appointed by Britain ruled Hong Kong. After 1997, a Chinese chief executive of the new SAR was appointed, the process being executed by an 800-strong electoral committee. The chief executive serves a five-year term and has the power to appoint a 13-member executive council that serves as a cabinet and advises on policy matters. There is also a 60-seat legislative council, elected by the people and business world of Hong Kong and certain key political players in Beijing.

Religious, cultural and historical influences

The principles of Taoism, Confucianism and Buddhism influence the people of Hong Kong, such that they have similar Chinese values to their counterparts on the mainland.

Historical Influences

Hong Kong has been a major trading port for centuries, and became embroiled in the Opium wars between China and Britain during the 19th Century. In 1898, a negotiated settlement between Britain and China saw Hong Kong island and its surrounding territories ceded to Britain under a 99-year lease. During this period Hong Kong was ruled by a British governor, until it was eventually returned to China in 1997.

In the days of British colonial rule, Hong Kong developed into a major financial and property development centre. It also became a trans-shipment point for the flow of goods into China.

For over a century Hong Kong Chinese have been exposed to British ways, and they are far more anglicised than their counterparts in the People's Republic. However with the influx of Chinese from the Mainland, the latent English culture that once existed is slowly disappearing.

Social and business values

As Hong Kong was a British colony for many years, some Chinese residents lead western lifestyles. In commerce they are more business minded and capitalistic than their counterparts in China, and hence more effective in concluding business deals. However, deep-rooted Chinese beliefs still dominate their ways in both society and business.

Local customs and etiquette

Special beliefs

The Chinese of Hong Kong practise the same beliefs as those living in China.

Etiquette

The same principles for China are applicable to Hong Kong.

Preparation and awareness

Appointment scheduling

Owing to the fact that most Hong Kong business people are quite westernised, requests for first-time appointments can be made in writing, by fax or via e-mail, to which replies should be promptly received. It is not necessary to rely on a personal introduction to initiate contact.

Business trips to Hong Kong can be scheduled at most times of the year, except for the period of the Chinese Lunar New Year. Between July and September, Hong Kong suffers from occasional typhoons (*tai wong*). When these are severe, businesses close for the duration of the typhoon (one to two days).

Business people of Hong Kong will expect visitors to arrive promptly for appointments. As Hong Kong Island, Kowloon and the New Territories do not cover a large area and the region is well served by a subway (MTR), travelling times between appointments should be relatively short and predictable. Note that when travelling by taxi, traffic jams may be encountered.

Gifts

The same Chinese principles for preparation and presentation of gifts apply to Hong Kong. However the following additional exclusions apply:

◻ Books – when pronounced in Cantonese, book sounds the same as "losing money". Books should therefore not be given to gamblers.

◻ Mirrors – in Hong Kong, asking someone to look at themselves in a mirror implies that he/she has too much pride.

During the 15 days of the Lunar New Year period, westerners who are well-acquainted with a Chinese person who has young unmarried children, can present them with a *lai see* ("red packet"). One packet is given for each child. They are red envelopes with Chinese writing into which money is placed. They can be obtained from most stationery stores. An even number of new, clean currency notes of even denomination should be placed in the packet – an amount in local currency equivalent to US$10 per child is usually sufficient. *Lai see* can also be given to the parents of a newborn child, to a bride and groom on their wedding day, or by companies to their staff over the Lunar New Year period.

Dress code

The dress code for Hong Kong is more formal than that of China. Men should wear suits with long-sleeved shirts and a tie. In the humid summer months, short-sleeved shirts and a tie are acceptable. Attire for women should also be more formal.

Name cards

As most business people in Hong Kong are able to read English, the need to have a name card printed in both English and Chinese is not essential, but will always be appreciated. If Chinese script is used, the classical form should be applied.

Meeting formalities

Names and forms of address

The same principles of name structure apply in Hong Kong as in China, where the family name appears first, followed by the given names. Many Chinese now also adopt a western given name. In such cases the adopted given name will appear first, followed by the family name. For example, it is quite clear that Jimmy Chan would be addressed formally as "Mr Chan", and as "Jimmy" in a less formal environment.

Meeting and greeting

The same protocols with regard to meeting and greeting in China apply in Hong Kong. A good impression will be created if a small bow is given when presenting name cards. This should be done just before shaking hands. A relaxed grip should be used, and pumping the other person's arm up and down avoided. It is more acceptable for a man to shake a woman's hand in Hong Kong, but again a light grip should be used.

Preliminaries

Meeting formalities in Hong Kong are similar to those that apply in China.

Negotiation etiquette

The Hong Kong Chinese, being more western oriented than those in China, are easier to deal with from an intercultural perspective. As Hong Kong business people have a higher command of English than people from China and Taiwan, they may appear more confident during negotiations. However they are extremely shrewd in business and are tough negotiators.

Meals and entertainment

Invitations

Most business entertainment in Hong Kong is undertaken in the evening, with dinner and after-dinner drinks being the norm. Lunch engagements are usually hurried affairs, as executives are keen to return to work.

Food and drink

Food in Hong Kong tends to be slightly sweeter and less spicy than that found in China. The same meal format used in China applies to Hong Kong.

Two popular forms of lighter meal entertainment in Hong Kong are tea drinking (*yum cha*) and *dim sum*. *Dim sum* is taken when only a quick light lunch is required, or traditionally as a "brunch" on Sunday mornings. The meal comprises a large number of small individual portions of mixed dumplings and pastries, containing minced pork, prawns, yam and red bean paste.

Table etiquette

Chinese meal etiquette applies in Hong Kong. When partaking of *yum cha* it is expected that drinkers will fill each other's cups. As a sign of appreciation, the receiver taps the three fingers of one hand on the table during the pouring process.

Although in China it is considered inappropriate to cross chopsticks, in *dim sum* restaurants in Hong Kong this is done to indicate that the meal is over and that the host is calling for the bill to be brought to the table.

Evening entertainment

As living space in Hong Kong is extremely tight and residential apartments are small and cramped, locals normally return home late at night, preferring to stay on longer at work or to frequent bars or night clubs. Thus time is often made for evening entertainment and, at the end of the meal, an invitation to go nightclubbing may sometimes be extended. It is advisable to accept such invitations.

Night spots are to be found throughout most of the city – the main Nathan Road in Kowloon area and the more salubrious Wanchai district on Hong Kong Island are two areas where foreigners may be entertained.

Republic of China – Taiwan (ROC)

Taiwan, also known as the Republic of China (ROC), is a mountainous island, situated south-east of mainland China. It also includes the Penghu Archipelago, a cluster of 64 islands. The country is unfortunately prone to frequent earth tremors and occasional earthquakes. Taiwan has the second highest population density in the world, slightly less than that of Bangladesh. Today, it is a major producer of high technology electronic goods and has the distinction of being the world's largest exporter of bicycles and fasteners (screws, nuts and bolts).

Since 1949, Taiwan has maintained a separate identity from China, and for this reason relationships between the two are strained. To visit the mainland, Taiwanese nationals require a special passport issued by China, while PRC citizens have difficulty in gaining approval to visit Taiwan. Recently, however, there have been signs of increasing co-operation, particularly with regards to Taiwan's investment on the mainland. To some extent the continuing political dissension between the two countries is probably related to nothing more than face-saving posturing.

Country background

Population

The population of Taiwan is 23 million. As the country is mountainous from the centre towards the East, most of the population is located along the western seaboard.

Ethnicity and religion

Almost the entire population of Taiwan is *Han* Chinese, originating from the southern coastal Chinese province of Fujian. Only 2% (approximately 400 000) are descendants of the original indigenous inhabitants. Over 90% of the population follow at least one or more of Confucian, Taoist or Buddhist beliefs, with five million people believed to be Buddhist. Christians comprise 5% of the population.

Language and script

Mandarin is the official spoken language of Taiwan, particularly in business circles. There is also a local Taiwanese dialect, Hokkien, spoken in rural areas. Hokkien has five tones while Mandarin has only four. The pictorial Chinese script used in Taiwan is the traditional form, and therefore may be interpreted differently from the newer script of China. Therefore, when translating any western text into Taiwanese script, a local translator should be used. Business people generally speak English, as it is taught in schools. However, outside the main business centres of Taipei and Kaohsiung, English comprehension may be quite poor, necessitating the services of an interpreter.

Taiwan has its own version of *Hanyu pin yin*, known as *Tong yung pin yin*. Pronunciation of most of the written English translations of Taiwanese proper nouns and names is quite straightforward, although some combinations of letters in *Tong yung pin yin* may cause confusion:

"HS", when followed by a vowel, is pronounced as "SH" with a slight sibilant sound. For example Hsinchu, a town in Taiwan, is pronounced "Shin-Chu", while Hsieng, a family name, as "Shieng".

"T" is pronounced with an emphasis on a "D" sound. For example Teng, a family name, is pronounced more like "TDeng".

"TS" is pronounced "CH". For example Tsai, a family name, is pronounced "Chai".

Regional structures

The country is divided into 16 provinces or counties (*Hsien*), each with its own governor and councils. *Hsien* are further divided into smaller regions known as *Hsiang*. In addition to this, seven of the larger cities, including Taipei (the capital and major financial centre) and Kaohsiung (the main industrial centre in the south), are classified as special municipalities.

Political environment

Taiwan is a constitutional democracy providing for a president, a National Assembly, and five *Yuan* that are responsible for executive, legislative, judicial and control functions. The executive *Yuan* (or cabinet, comprising all the appointed ministers) is the highest body of the five, and is headed by the premier, who is appointed by the president. Full democratic elections have only been held since 1994. The president is elected by the populace and serves a four-year term.

The two main political parties of Taiwan are the original Chinese National Party – Kuomintang (KMT) initiated by the Chiang family, and the Democratic Progressive Party (DPP). The KMT supports the view that Taiwan and China should be more united, while the DPP takes the more radical stance that Taiwan should remain independent. In the south the DPP enjoys greater support as this region is home to indigenous inhabitants, who have always considered themselves free from China.

Religious, cultural and historical influences

As in China, Taoism, Confucianism and Buddhism influence the ways of the Taiwanese.

Historical Influences

Although for many centuries Taiwan was a neglected protectorate of the Chinese Empire, it was the Portuguese who discovered it in 1590, naming it Ilha Formosa, meaning "Beautiful Island". Formosa remained the country's name in the western world for many centuries afterwards.

During the 17th century the Dutch East India Company briefly adopted it as a trading base. In 1895 Japan invaded Taiwan and ruled it for nearly 40 years, until its defeat at the end of the Second World War.

Shortly after the war, in 1949, following the defeat of Chiang Kai Shek's Nationalist Kuomintang party (KMT) in China by Mao Zedong's Communist forces, Chiang fled to Taiwan, where he established a new one-party government and imposed martial law.

In 1971, Taiwan lost its membership of the United Nations, as a condition imposed by China when it agreed to join the UN. Since then Taiwan has been able to enjoy relations with only a limited number of countries.

Martial law was eventually lifted in 1987. The first direct elections were only held in 1996.

Despite being considerably smaller than the mainland, some Taiwanese still regard their country as "the real China" and view China as a part of Taiwan. Others claim that Taiwan should be entirely independent of China. Needless to say, the converse view is held by China, which considers Taiwan to be a renegade state.

Despite the ongoing friction between the two countries, Taiwan has been successful in establishing many factories throughout China, with many Taiwanese living on the mainland.

Social and business values

Taiwanese are generally friendly and hospitable. This trait is more prevalent in the south around Kaohsiung. As Japan dominated Taiwan for 50 years, many older Taiwanese still exhibit strong Japanese traits, such as obedience, loyalty and punctuality. Japanese culture and ways are appreciated, because unlike elsewhere in Asia, less brutality was practised against the local population during the periods of Japanese occupation.

In more recent times, American culture has been imported into Taiwan, as many of the younger generation are sent to study in the United States and upon returning home bring with them American influences.

Owing to their isolation from China and many other countries in the world, Taiwanese have had to fend for themselves. They have over time developed into a highly innovative culture, particularly in the areas of high technology and electronics. They have a remarkable ability to expand basic research and development concepts into successful and competitive full-scale production facilities.

Like the Chinese from Hong Kong, Taiwanese are more capitalistic and business-minded than their counterparts on the mainland. Owing to the fact that many of them have been exposed to the West through overseas education, they are always willing to explore new business opportunities. They tend to spend less time on preliminary relationship-building formalities before getting down to business matters. In their endeavours to consummate business deals they appear more brusque and arrogant than the Chinese on the mainland. They value co-operation and are flexible in their approach to problems. Taiwanese have a strong work ethic, and tend to work longer hours than many people from western countries.

Local customs and etiquette

Special beliefs

The Chinese of Taiwan practise the same beliefs as those of China.

Etiquette

The same principles of inappropriate behaviour found in China are applicable to Taiwan. Conversation about communism and differences between Taiwan and China should be avoided.

Preparation and awareness

Appointment scheduling

Requests for appointments with Taiwanese can be made directly in writing. There should not be a need to initiate contact though third-party personal links, as is the case in China.

In Taiwan, the Lunar New Year is a prime holiday period, this being the only time when travel to the country should be avoided. Most businesses close during the week after the first day of the New Year. Taiwan does not recognise or celebrate the National Day of China, held in October. Like Hong Kong, Taiwan suffers from typhoons between July and September, and business may be suspended for a day or two during severe conditions.

With the focus of attention of many business enterprises now turning to China, Taiwanese executives are also spending more of their time away and may not always be available for appointments. Sometimes a key person may have to postpone or cancel a meeting at short notice, owing to an urgent need to rush off to China.

Although traffic congestion in Taipei, the capital of Taiwan used to be atrocious, the situation has recently improved. Despite this, when scheduling appointments ample time should be provided to reach a destination, as traffic jams still occur. The Taiwanese, along with most other Chinese cultures, expect visitors to be punctual.

Gifts

The basic rules in selecting gifts for Chinese people apply in Taiwan. The Taiwanese tend to be more generous in the gifts they present, so it is advisable to prepare gifts of a higher standard than usual. Gifts that have been made in Taiwan or China should be avoided. A special item from a home country or a bottle of wine or spirits is always suitable.

Dress code

In the major centres of Taiwan, a jacket, long-sleeved shirt and tie is recommended for men. During the hot months of June to September, it is permissible to wear a short-sleeved shirt and tie, without a jacket, which is only required for more formal meetings with senior people. In outlying industrial areas no jacket or tie are necessary. Women may wear normal business attire as they would in the West, although short skirts should be avoided.

Name cards

As most business people in Taiwan are able to read English, the need to have name cards printed in both English and Chinese is not essential, but will always be appreciated. Any special titles or academic qualifications should be displayed.

Meeting formalities

Names and forms of address

Taiwanese personal names follow the Chinese order of family name first, followed by two given names. The latter may often be hyphenated. When printing their name cards in English, Taiwanese sometimes place their hyphenated given names in front of their family name. For example, Chung-chen Wu is formally addressed "Mr Wu", and informally as "Chung-chen". The correct word order for his name should be Wu Chung-chen.

The western "Mr" and "Mrs", or "Ms", is used in Taiwan. However, when addressing high-ranking executives or government officials, it is more appropriate to use their title. For instance, if Mr Wu happened to be the chairman of a large corporation, he should be addressed as "Chairman Wu", particularly in written communication.

Meeting and greeting

The same protocols with regard to meeting and greeting in China, apply in Taiwan.

Preliminaries

Meeting formalities in Taiwan are similar to those of China.

Negotiation etiquette

Taiwanese businessmen tend to be extremely tough negotiators on matters such as price, and where possible will usually take the lowest offer, with little regard for other value-adding components such as quality and service. They are experts at biding time to wear down the patience of the opposing negotiating party, and may intentionally delay accepting an offer for as long as possible in the hope that the other party will become impatient and hurriedly make further concessions. Advantage may also be taken of unethical exploitation of Chinese values. For instance, requests for lower prices in order "for me to save face with my boss" or "to keep the relationship going" are not uncommon in Taiwan.

During meetings, Taiwanese negotiators often talk among themselves in Mandarin or Taiwanese, taking advantage of foreigners' inability to comprehend their language. In so doing they are cunningly able to formulate tactics for the next stages of the discussions. Such actions can be limited by bringing an interpreter to the meeting.

Meals and entertainment

Invitations

Most business entertainment in Taiwan is done in the evening, with dinner and after-dinner drinks being the norm. Where time permits, invitations to such events should be accepted. Lunch engagements are usually hurried affairs, as executives are under pressure to return to work as quickly as possible.

Food and drink

Taiwanese food is similar to that found in China. The chances of being served an unpalatable dish in Taiwan are quite low, although snake dishes are quite common.

Alcohol is an integral and major part of most dinners. Normally, beer is served first, followed by red wine. Sometimes local "yellow" wine of a low alcohol content may also be served (*Shao Hsing* wine). Higher alcohol-bearing liquor, *wu liang ye* ("five grain liquor") or *Kaoliang*, the Taiwanese equivalent of PRC's *baijiu* may also be served, usually in small liqueur glasses. These contain in excess of 50% alcohol and should be consumed with caution. An expensive vintage whisky may also be offered on completion of the meal. The result is that diners end up with numerous glasses of different forms of alcohol, as well as a cup of green Chinese tea! The usual Chinese custom of frequent toasting (*ganbei*) is also practised in Taiwan. Those vulnerable to the after-effects of mixing drinks should therefore proceed with care.

Table etiquette

Meal etiquette as practised in China also applies to Taiwan.

Evening entertainment

Time is often made for evening entertainment, and on conclusion of the meal an invitation to go nightclubbing will be extended. It is recommended that invitations to these activities are accepted.

Two popular nightlife areas to visit in Taipei are the Hsinyi and Jhongshan districts. Hsinyi is a modern part of Taiwan dominated by the 508m-high Taipei 101 Tower, named after its 101 stories – in 2006 it was the tallest building in the world. A magnificent view of the hills surrounding Taipei can be had from the 89th level.

Many trendy and expensive restaurants can be found in and around Taipei 101. The Jhongshan district is full of nightclubs and *Karoake* bars and has remnants of Japanese forms of entertainment. An interesting feature of this area are "barber shops". While on the outside they may appear to be places where men can get their hair cut, they are actually fronts for massage parlours offering a wide range of services, from simple massages to much more! One should therefore be circumspect when receiving an invitation to one of these establishments.

5 Thailand

Roughly the same size as France, Thailand comprises a mainland with a broad mountainous northern area, extending down to a narrow lowland region in the south, on the Malay peninsula. Also found in this area are hundreds of small resort islands for which the country is famous.

Thailand means "land of the free" and is one of the few countries in Asia that has not been colonised by the West. Foreigners from most countries are always welcome, with tourism being a major industry. Thai etiquette also applies to the Indochina countries on its borders, namely Laos, Cambodia and Myanmar. All these countries have been founded on Buddhist beliefs, which largely determine the basic principles by which the people of this region live. Although the country largely comprises ethnic Thais, there is a small complement of Chinese immigrants. This group also practises its own beliefs, in addition to Thai customs, which sometimes makes it difficult to distinguish Thai-Chinese from ethnic Thai.

Country background

Population
The population of Thailand is 63 million.

Ethnicity and religion
About 77% of the populace is ethnic Thai, split into four basic groups, each with its own dialect. Of the population 12% is of Chinese origin (Thai-Chinese) and 6% is Muslim, found mainly in the south, on the northern border of the Islamic country Malaysia. Muslim minorities are also found in the north, having migrated from China during the 19th century. *Theravada* Buddhism is practised by 94% of the population.

Language and script
The Thai alphabet comprises 44 consonant characters with 25 "vowels" (five vowels each with five tones). Letters are written in a form of Sanskrit. The language is difficult to grasp as it is tonal, with some words having five tones, each conveying a different meaning.

Thai words, when translated into the western alphabet, can easily be pronounced, although the following special cases apply:

When a consonant is followed by an "h", it is silent.

"Th" is pronounced as a hard "T" e.g. the city name Thon Buri is pronounced "Ton Buri".

"Ph" is pronounced as a hard "P" e.g. Phuket is pronounced "Poo-ket". The islands of Phi Phi are pronounced "Pee Pee".

"U" is pronounced as a "OO" e.g. Khrung Thep, the Thai name for Bangkok, is pronounced "Kroong Tep".

The letters "K" and "G" are sometimes interchangeable, with a hard "K" substituting a "G" and vice versa.

Thais also have a way of pronouncing the letter "R", like an "L". For instance three may be heard as "tlee".

Owing to the fact that the education system is good and given that Thailand's key tourism industry is targeted at the European market, most Thai people across the country comprehend English reasonably well, provided it is spoken slowly.

Regional structures

Thailand is divided into 75 provinces, each controlled by a governor. In addition to this, the Bangkok metropolitan area is treated as a separate administrative area.

Political environment

Thailand is one of few countries in the world, and the only one in Asia, existing as a kingdom with a true monarch. The Thai monarchy can be traced back to the 13th century, the Sukhothai period. The present king, Bhumibol Adulyadej (Rama IX, born in 1927), has been the longest reigning monarch, ascending to the throne in 1946 at the age of 18.

A true democratic constitution has been in existence since 1932. There is a prime minister and a parliament with two legislative houses, an upper (House of Senators with 200 members) and a lower (House of Representatives with 500 members). The House of Representatives elects the prime minister. The party system in Thailand over the past ten years has experienced frequent changes to names and structures. In 2006 the four dominant political parties were the ruling party of Prime Minister Thaksin, Thai Rak Thai ("Thais love Thais"), the Democratic party, Chart Thai and Mahachon. Following a peaceful military coup over Thaksin's corrupt ways, a caretaker prime minister was installed, with fresh elections due in 2007.

Religious, cultural and historical influences

As with most other south-east Asian countries, there is a significant presence of Chinese ways in Thailand. These are however overshadowed by the customs of the local Thai people, whose dominant religion is Buddhism. Islamic beliefs prevail in the southern portions of the country. Coupled with this, Shamanism or spirit belief also plays a significant role in shaping Thai culture.

Ethnic boundaries

The Thai-Chinese group aligns itself with Thai cultural ways, such that it may be difficult for westerners to tell them apart from ethnic Thais. As most Chinese in Thailand have assumed Thai names, it is not possible to use this as a means by which to identify them. However, ethnic Thais can be distinguished from Thai-Chinese in that the latter tend to have a lighter skin colour. Ethnic Thais will be found working for state companies or big corporations, whereas in small private business Thai-Chinese will predominate.

Buddhism

The principle belief of Buddhism is that human beings pass through a series of reincarnations. The orthodox or *Theravada* form of Buddhism emerged in Thailand around 300 BC with the arrival of Indian merchants and monks. *Theravada* followers believe that after passing through a number of reincarnations they too eventually become Buddhas. Followers frequently practise prayer rituals (a form of meditation) to images of Buddha in temples and shrines. The abundance of many traditional temples throughout Thailand bears testimony to this. Since Buddhism is strongly ingrained in the country, males, prior to turning 25, strive to enter a monastery and become a monk for at least three months.

The Spirit World (Shamanism)

Thai people also believe in Shamanism or spirit worship. This involves paying homage to the souls of departed human beings, while seeking their advice. Small charms or figurines depicting Buddha are worn around the neck, displayed in cars and around the house, to ward off malevolent spirits. So-called guardian spirits are those which supposedly protect homes and businesses.

Most Thai-Chinese and Thais practise both Shamanism and *Theravada* Buddhism. This is evidenced by the presence of both Buddhist and spirit-house shrines that are erected outside the entrances of dwellings, where they stand side by side. The Buddhist shrine is larger, housing an image of Buddha, while the spirit house is much smaller, containing figurines. These icons are symbolic of the Thai outlook that relies on both Buddha and the spirits to guide them forward in life.

Historical Influences

Evidence dating back to the Bronze Age indicates that Thailand was inhabited at this time. Thailand's recorded history began after the birth of Christ, following the arrival of Chinese insurgents. Further immigration of Chinese (Khmers) from southern China, as a result of forced eviction by the Han Chinese, occurred during the 11th century. Thereafter the Khmers ruled the country.

In 1767 Thailand was overrun for a few months by its neighbour, Burma (now Myanmar), before the locals successfully expelled the Burmese. To this day, Thailand is still wary of such invasions. Shortly afterwards a constitutional monarchy was established. The King of Thailand is a key figurehead in the lives of all modern Thai people.

Japan invaded Thailand during the Second World War, but left following its defeat by the Allied forces in Asia Pacific in 1945.

Thailand was the centre of the Asian crisis in 1997, when many south-east Asian countries found their economies in tatters as a result of large US-dollar debts that could not be paid. President Thaksin Shinawatra (elected in 2001) initiated an economic recovery by applying business principles to run the country as a corporate conglomerate. He was ousted by a peaceful military coup in 2006 following allegations of corruption and tax evasion.

Social and business values

As with most other Asian cultures, Thais show respect to superiors, teachers and the elderly. The ethnic Thai outlook is to enjoy a carefree and pleasant existence. A simple life of contentment is preferred to one of materialism, while maximising enjoyment of the small things in life. To them, life must be fun or in their vernacular, *sanuk*. Every undertaking, whether it be visiting friends or fulfilling a task, should be *sanuk*. The words *sabai sabai* are used to signify happiness and contentment. Actions are geared towards an avoidance of conflict and a desire to please. Thai-Chinese, on the other hand, like to make money and show off their wealth through material possessions and indulgence in luxury.

An important facet of life is the "Thai smile" which is used to alleviate embarrassing situations or to avoid loud arguments. It is no surprise, therefore, that Thailand is known as the "Land of Smiles". Thais have a remarkable capacity for patience and tolerance, which means that tasks may not always be completed on time.

Should the outcome of an event not happen as expected, Thais accept this situation philosophically, adopting the attitude *mai phen rai* ("such is life"). This can be very frustrating for westerners, whose first reaction under stress might be to vent anger. Self-control (*chai yen yen*) in times of stress should be practised, as although Thais are usually extremely tolerant, outlandish behaviour can make them extremely uncooperative.

Thai people hold the monarchy in esteem, and love and cherish their king. In most offices a picture of the king can be seen hanging in the reception area. Westerners should also show respect to members of the Thai monarchy. In addition to the national anthem of Thailand, the king also has his own national anthem. Whenever this is played it is absolutely essential that everyone, including foreigners, stand up as a sign of respect.

Compared to other Asian cultures, Thais are far more tolerant of westerners. This originates from their Buddhist beliefs and their desire that life's encounters be *sanuk*. Although they will be warm, friendly and receptive, there is still a strong requirement for relationship building within the Thai business environment.

Local Thais call westerners, *farang*. This originates from early arrivals of French people who were believed to be the first Caucasians to visit Thailand. The word *farang* refers to their brown hair. Interestingly, *farang* is also the Thai word for the guava fruit! Fortunately, it is not used in a derogatory manner.

From street-side vendors to the business world, Thais are keen to bargain and extensive negotiation should be expected. Locals believe that westerners are very wealthy and therefore charge over-inflated prices in shops and stores. There is usually a two-tier system of pricing – the "local price" and a much higher "foreign price". A commercial offer originating from a Thai firm may therefore contain a significant "foreign price" component.

Despite the Buddhism tenets of preaching a clean and pure life, business ways in Thailand do not always follow the same principles. Situations may arise where dubious requests are made to secure a business deal. The recommendations of spirits in Thai decision-making should also not be underestimated. Spirits may be consulted for advice on a key decision, and also on matters pertaining to the timing of new ventures and project start-ups.

Local customs and etiquette

Special beliefs

Western visitors to Thailand should be aware of the following special beliefs:

- Even numbers are generally considered unlucky, while odd numbers, such as three and five, are lucky. Nine is especially lucky because in Thai it sounds the same as the expression for "step forward". Four is considered extremely unlucky, as it is associated with death.
- White is not a preferred colour, as it is associated with funerals.
- The head of a person is considered most sacred, while the foot of a person is seen as unholy.
- The elephant is revered amongst the Thais, as it has played a significant role in past years as a workhorse and means of transport.
- Loss of temper is seen as a severe social lapse.
- Images of Buddha, once monks have blessed them, are considered sacrosanct. Export of such sacred figures from Thailand is illegal.
- Monks wearing saffron-coloured robes enjoy special status. Certain protocols apply when greeting them and passing objects to them. Seats in trains and buses are often reserved for monks.
- Great respect is shown at all times to the king and all images of him.

Etiquette

When interacting with Thais **don't**:

- Outwardly show anger or shout in times of stress.
- Touch any person, even young children, on the head.
- Touch or display any form of affection to a Thai woman in public, except to shake hands.
- Point to or push an object on the ground, with the foot.
- Cross the legs when seated in the presence of others, where the foot of the crossed leg points towards the head of someone else, and particularly that of an elder or more senior person. Care should be taken that the foot does not inadvertently point towards a religious image or picture of the king.
- Throw items across to a person.
- Present items such as name cards, gifts, cash and credit cards using the left hand; use only the right hand or both hands.

- Belittle the king or deface images of him.
- Mishandle or desecrate the Thai currency, as this depicts the monarch. In particular do not stand on it, or place the currency in a shoe or sock, as might be done for safekeeping.
- Use a crooked index finger to beckon someone; rather use the standard Asian method of palm down and flapping the hand.
- Step over the legs or body of someone seated or lying on the ground – walk around them and bow deferentially while passing by.
- Discuss Mynanmar (Burma), as friction still exists between these two countries.
- Touch Buddha figurines or amulets, particularly those worn around the neck.
- Touch a monk. This rule applies particularly to women.
- Sit next to a monk on a train or a bus, if you happen to be female.
- Sit with your head higher than that of a monk.

Preparation and awareness

Appointment scheduling

As Thailand is well aligned with the ways of the West, establishing contact for the first time via a direct approach should be relatively easy. Responses to requests for appointments made by e-mail or fax can be expected.

It is advisable not to schedule appointments in Thailand during the following holiday periods:

- Songkhran, or water festival (around 13th April)
  This is a period where for three days many Thais return home to pay their respects to family elders. This exacerbates traffic jams, increasing travel times even further. Thai business counterparts may simply be unavailable at this time, because of the holiday period. As this is the hottest period in Thailand, tradition permits the drenching of anyone, *farangs* included, with water. This can be administered either by bucket or high-powered water pistol. Needless to say, victims of such an assault should remember to smile!
- Chinese New Year (January/February – lunar-based)
  Businesses run by Thai-Chinese citizens may be closed over the Chinese New Year period.

Although the construction of more freeways and rail transit systems in recent years has eased traffic congestion, it still remains a problem as car ownership is increasing. Additional time should be allowed between meetings to cater for delays arising from traffic jams. When Thais are asked how long it takes to reach a destination such as the airport, they will always overstate the time, on the assumption that there will be a lengthy traffic jam along the way. It is recommended that hotels be chosen with care, so that they are close to appointment venues. Congestion in the main city areas, such as Sukhumvit, can cause tremendous delays, particularly during rush-hour periods. A new breed of taxi driver is emerging in Thailand. These individuals have a poor command of English and are often not familiar with the correct route to a given address – this should be written down in Thai. If a busy city schedule is anticipated, prepare to hire a hotel car with an English-speaking driver, on an hourly rate.

Thais generally arrive on time for meetings, but are tolerant of visitors who arrive late because of the traffic delays.

Gifts

In Thailand, gifts are not usually given at the first meeting, but it is a good idea to have gifts available, in case there is a need to reciprocate. Thais also celebrate the western New Year, by giving New Year's cards and food hampers to business partners or customers.

The following guidelines apply when choosing gifts for ethnic Thais:
- Where a gift comprises more than one of the same item, an odd rather than even number of items should be given.
- It is acceptable to give flowers (an odd number), but marigolds and carnations should be avoided, as these are associated with funerals.
- White gift-wrapping should not be used, as this colour is associated with funerals. Most other colours are suitable.
- It is acceptable to give alcohol (especially brandy), wallets, purses and pens.

In situations where a recipient is Thai-Chinese, gifts considered inappropriate among the Chinese community should be avoided. These include:
- Clocks (a sign that death is near).
- Knives, scissors or letter-openers (represents a cut in the relationship).
- Socks, sandals, handkerchiefs and towels (associated with funerals and grieving).
- Food items should not be presented at the end of a meal to the host, as this implies that the meal was insufficient.

An acceptable gift for an important Chinese person is a bottle of expensive brandy, as this is a popular drink at home. Red wine is also appropriate as Chinese consider it healthy for the heart, while its colour brings prosperity.

Gifts should be wrapped in brightly coloured paper, preferably in red or yellow. If red paper is used, the red colour should not be too dominant. Purple and white paper should not be used, as in Taoism these are associated with funerals. An unwrapped gift should not be presented, as this is considered impolite.

Dress code

During normal business hours, men need not always wear a jacket, but a long-sleeved shirt (preferably white) and tie are recommended. As the climate is hot and humid, lightweight clothing is advisable. When attending a formal event or meeting very senior people, a jacket or suit is required.

Women should wear attire with short or long sleeves. Sleeveless or skimpy tops and short skirts are not acceptable. Black is not a good colour to wear as this is associated with funerals, although it is perfectly acceptable for evening functions.

If it is anticipated that temple visiting will be part of the itinerary, a pair of shoes that can easily be slipped on and off should be worn.

Name cards

As English is well understood in business circles, it is not necessary to have name cards or promotional literature printed in the local script.

Meeting formalities

Names and forms of address

Thai names usually comprise two words, with the family name appearing last. The family name is usually the longest and more complicated of the two and in many instances can be extremely difficult to pronounce. Before the 20th century, Thais only had given names, but later, the ruling King Rama VI decreed that family names be adopted. When registering their new names, many people opted for names that were unique and had grandiose meanings, best accomplished by the use of lengthy words. Today, names implying excellence, wealth, progress and prosperity predominate. Fortunately, Thais are called by their given names, which are shorter and much easier to pronounce. Although Thais can be addressed as Mr or Ms {given name}, the Thai salutation is *Khun*, and is the same for both male and female. Thus a man with the name Boonlert Chernsiridumrong will be addressed as "Khun Boonlert". Once a closer relationship has been developed, the *Khun* prefix can be dropped and the person called by their first name.

As the Thai salutation of *Khun* is the same for both men and women, it is impossible for westerners to determine the gender of a person from their name. As many women occupy management positions in Thai companies, do not assume that a person that you are about to meet for the first time will be male.

In less formal environments, and as an aid to westerners, some Thais use a single syllable nickname (e.g. "Tee"). In this case it will not be necessary to use the *Khun* prefix. On marriage, Thai women normally assume their husband's family name, although in the Thai-Chinese context this may not always occur.

Although there are many Thai-Chinese operating in the business environment, they often have Thai names, in order to maintain a Thai identity and also as a result of intermarriage with ethnic Thais. It may be difficult to identify a Thai-Chinese person from their name. In some cases, though, the first few letters of a family name bear phonetic resemblance to the Chinese clan name. For instance in Thai, the original Chinese family name Chong would appear as Chongchananathi.

Meeting and greeting

Although Thais do not generally shake hands among themselves, this practice is becoming more acceptable and is common in business circles, particularly when westerners are present. The traditional form of Thai greeting is the *wai*, pronounced "why". This symbolises the giving of a budding Lotus flower, a sign of Buddhist enlightenment. This greeting is not only used to bid welcome or farewell, but also as a sign of respect and thanks.

The *wai* is executed by placing the hands together, palm to palm, with the fingers together and the fingertips pointing up, at a level between the mouth and nose. There are variations of the *wai* depending upon the degree of respect that is accorded. Most respect is shown to a monk, a Buddha image or the king. In this case the hands are raised to above eye level, with the thumbs placed at the top of the nose bridge between the eyebrows and fingertips, touching the hairline. When greeting a senior member of the family, an elderly person or a teacher, the thumbs should touch the tip of the nose and the fingertips the space between the eyebrows. In the case of other respected people, the hands are raised such that the thumbs touch the chin and the fingertips touch the tip of the nose. The above actions may be accompanied by a slight bowing of the head and body. The head bow is accentuated when greeting people of higher status, particularly monks.

It is customary among locals to *rap wai* by way of acknowledgement. The pressed palms are placed such that the thumbs are at chest level and the fingertips at the chin, with a slight bow of the head.

When meeting a person commanding respect (such as a customer), a person of lower status (such as someone in a service-related function) will initiate a *wai*. The more senior person is not obliged to reciprocate, and need only acknowledge the greeting with a slight nod of the head.

Many foreigners visiting Thailand tend to use the *wai*, when actually this is not really necessary. It is acceptable for foreigners to merely acknowledge a *wai* from a person of lower status, with a nod of the head and a smile. It is however expected that everyone, regardless of origin or nationality, should *wai* a monk. Owing to their status, monks are not expected to *rap wai*.

When western women meet Thai males, they should initiate a handshake. Failing this they may be given a *wai*, in which case they should reciprocate in the same way. Traditionally when greeting Thai women, men should *wai* them. However, in today's environment, Thai women may well initiate a handshake. Handshakes with Thais are normally executed briefly and with a soft grip.

Name cards are exchanged using the two-handed technique, with the text aligned the right way up for the receiver. Time should be taken to study the owner's details, and if necessary to enquire about their background. There might be occasions where Thai given names appear amusing to westerners – it is wise to avoid making any inappropriate comments.

Preliminaries

Formalities and etiquette in Thai business meetings are similar to those of the West. As practised in most Asian countries, guests take their places at the meeting table, such that they face the entrance of the room. Sometimes, first meetings may be held over lunch or dinner where very little business may be discussed. This should be seen as an opportunity to develop favourable relationships.

Negotiation etiquette

In Thailand, meetings with foreigners are usually conducted in English. Pidgin English should be avoided, as this may be perceived as insulting. Expect members of the Thai group to communicate among themselves in their own language.

During negotiations, if the Thai party feels uncomfortable making an immediate decision, an evasive response may be forthcoming – replies such as "Let us see' and "We have to refer this to someone else" are such examples. Needless to say if there are any moments of embarrassment, these will be covered up with laughter or a smile. Western negotiators should try to maintain a calm, pleasant demeanour at all times during stressful sessions.

Meals and entertainment

Invitations

A dinner invitation may be extended, once business has finished for the day. Where possible such invitations should be accepted. Thais try to hold business dinners fairly early in the evening, almost immediately after the close of business. It is customary for partners to be included. While it is quite common in the West to hold breakfast meetings, lunch and dinner meetings are preferred in Thailand.

Food and drink

The chances are western visitors will be invited to a restaurant serving Thai food. If the hosts happen to be Thai-Chinese, then a Chinese restaurant will probably be selected, where the menu may have spicy Thai variations.

Food in Thai restaurants is usually quite "safe" in that strange or unpalatable dishes are uncommon. Thai food is well known for being spicy. Ingredients such as chilli, peppercorns, lemon grass and coconut milk are used to create flavours that are unique to Thailand.

Knowledge of these few Thai words will help foreigners to find their way around a Thai menu: prawns are *goong*, chicken is *gai*, pork is *moo*, beef is *nua* and fish, *pla*. Rice is known as *kao* and local noodles (a semi-transparent or "glassy " vermicelli) are called *guay*. Fried rice is *kao pad*.

There is a myriad of different dishes to be found in Thailand, with the most common being:

- *Tom yum goong* and *tom yum gai*: considered Thailand's signature dishes, these are extremely spicy soups containing vegetables, lotus root and either prawns or chicken.
- *Tom kha gai*: a creamy version of *tom yum gai*, made with coconut milk and containing a type of ginger known as *galangal*.
- *Kaeng kiew wan* (*nua, gai* or *goong*): a spicy curry in the form of a casserole, made with green curry paste and coconut milk.
- *Kaeng phed* is the same as *Kaeng kiew*, except that it is made with red curry paste.

◻ *Kao pad subparod* is fried rice mixed with shrimps, chicken and pineapple pieces, served in a pineapple shell. This is a good safe option for foreigners in that it is very tasty and not spicy.

Thailand is also famous for its spicy salads (*tam som*), and the most popular of these contain grapefruit or papaya.

Dessert is normally a simple affair, consisting of cut fruit and traditional Thai desserts, such as small cakes and jellies.

Thais do not consider drinking at meal times as essential for relationship-building. However, when dealing with Thai-Chinese, drinking is used far more in relationship-building, where red wine is usually the preferred beverage. *Saeng thip*, a brown coloured rice liqueur containing 40% alcohol is the local liquor. It has a slightly sweet taste, and is usually mixed with water or soda in a long glass. This drink is not normally offered to foreigners.

Table etiquette

Settings in Thai restaurants can be around either a circular or a rectangular table. If a private room has been hired, the usual etiquette dictates that the most important guest is seated to the right of the host, facing the door. In northern Thailand, a traditional meal may be taken seated on the floor.

The format of Thai dining follows that of Chinese meals, where communal dishes are served from which diners help themselves. At the beginning of the meal, rice is served onto each diner's plate and is eaten along with servings selected from the communal dishes.

Eating utensils are a fork and spoon, unless a Chinese meal or Thai noodles are being eaten, in which case chopsticks will be used. For the right-handed person, the fork is held in the left hand and the spoon in the right (vice versa for left-handers). The correct way to eat is to push food onto the spoon with the fork, and eat with the spoon. The side of the spoon can be used as a knife to cut food into smaller pieces.

Towards the end of the meal, a host may offer the last serving to the most important guest, as a sign of honour. It is considered polite to initially decline this, but after further persuasion the food should be accepted.

Table etiquette dictates that:

◻ The American manner of rotating the fork and using it to shovel food into the mouth should be avoided – Thais perceive this as an unacceptable manner of eating.

◻ Soup should not be consumed by lifting the bowl and drinking from it as would be done in Japan – a spoon should be used in the normal western manner. It is also considered impolite to slurp when eating soup.

◻ At the end of the meal it is advisable to leave a small amount on the plate to signify that one is replete.

Evening entertainment

Thailand has a myriad of nightspots promoting interesting forms of entertainment for male travellers. In various guises, these blatantly offer fraternisation with local women, ranging from *Karaoke* lounges, hostess bars and Thai massage parlours. Foreign male visitors may be invited to one of these after dinner. While providing a good opportunity for relationship-building, care should be exercised as to how far these are pursued. The safest option is to limit the entertainment to *Karaoke* and drinking.

Thailand is famous for the "Thai massage", which is administered in a number of ways. A relaxing massage using the Thai method of applying pressure with the fingers and elbows to reduce muscle stress is known as a "Traditional Thai Massage". This is a perfectly safe and normal type of massage that both men and women can enjoy, obtainable at most advertised parlours where trained staff are at hand. However, there is also the "Thai massage" or "Modern massage", which is nothing more than an offer of sexual favours. It is therefore recommended that when invited for a "massage", the nature of the service be established so that compromising situations can be avoided. No loss of face or offence will be taken if such an invitation is declined.

6　Japan

Japan comprises over 3 000 islands, the four largest being Hokkaido, Honshu (the main island on which the business centres of Tokyo and Osaka are located), Shikoku and Kyushu.

The people of Japan originate from a number of Asian cultures, creating a culture with a unique and interesting set of values and beliefs. In the past the Japanese way has been to protect the country and preserve beliefs by maintaining a protected "bubble" environment. As Japan is an aggressive global foreign investor, and most Japanese are avid overseas holidaymakers, many opportunities exist for interaction with westerners. Unlike most south-east Asian countries, there are no significant enclaves of Chinese people in Japan. Chinese beliefs that were transferred to Japan many centuries ago have been absorbed into an almost homogeneous culture.

Country background

Population

The population of Japan is 128 million, 70% of which live on the four main islands. From 2006 the population is predicted to decline owing to the low birth rate of the country.

Ethnicity and religion

The majority (99.4%) of the population is ethnic Japanese and 0.5% is Korean. Inhabitants of the northern islands have Korean origins and tend to be taller than those of the south, who come from Taiwan and as far afield as Polynesia.

Over 75% of Japanese follow one of many forms of Buddhism found in the country. There is also a widespread, ingrained belief in Shinto ways. Although many younger Japanese claim to have no single religion, many practise both Buddhist and Shinto ways. Christians comprise 4% of the population.

Language and script

The local language is unique to Japan, with over 60 dialects being spoken across the country. Unlike Chinese and Thai, Japanese is not tonal.

While spoken Japanese is relatively easy to learn, it is much more difficult to comprehend the written form. Important names, such as those of hotels, Japanese personal names etc, are displayed in *kanji*, which are Chinese characters. For this reason, Chinese people can get around quite easily by following signs displayed in the local script. In addition to *kanji*, two other alphabets are used, known as *hiragana* and *katakana*. *Hiragana* is a local script used for common words and text, while *katakana* is applied to depict modern words, such as technical terms and foreign names. A westerner's name when translated into Japanese will invariably be shown in *katakana*. The three scripts can be identified by their appearance. *Kanji* assumes the typical complex and pictorial character of Chinese script, *hiragana* is simpler, having rounded and Cyrillic characters, while *katakana* is more angular and straight-lined. It is possible to find all three types of script in one sentence. *Hiragana* and *katakana* each have 50 characters. The basics of *kanji* on the other hand embrace more than 4 000 pictorial symbols. As in the case of classic Chinese text, Japanese writing is usually read in columns from right to left, meaning that books and magazines are seen to be read backwards.

Japanese vowels are pronounced differently from those of the West:

a is pronounced as in c<u>a</u>rd

e is pronounced as in <u>e</u>ver

i is pronounced as in m<u>ee</u>t

o is pronounced as in l<u>o</u>w

u is pronounced as in r<u>u</u>le

Where two vowels are adjacent to each other they are pronounced separately, whereas in the West they would be pronounced as a single syllable. For example, Japanese pronounce the word "cried" as "cree–ed", separating the two vowel sounds. The Japanese name "Toshio" is pronounced "Toh–shi–oh".

Japanese grammar structures are more complicated, in that sentence construction is based on the importance of the person being addressed. Higher levels of politeness are used when speaking to an elder or more senior person, apologising and when an important request is being made. This honorific form of address is known as *keigo*, and requires the use of different vocabulary and grammar to that of less formal environments. There are at least four different levels of politeness. As the need to speak more politely increases, so does the complexity and indirectness of a sentence. Women were previously expected to use more deferential forms of speech when addressing men, but now in modern Japan this is no longer the case. While older women may still follow the tradition, young women of today use almost the same form of speech as men.

The Japanese counting system uses the value of 10 000 (*man*) as a basic unit for expressing large numbers, such as millions and billions. In converting a number from their language to English, some Japanese may lose or gain a zero in the translation. To avoid any misunderstandings, it is recommended that you double-check numbers by expressing them in writing.

Regional structures

Japan is divided into 47 prefectures, or *ken*, which are modelled on the French system.

Political environment

Japan has an elected prime minister and democratic government, comprising a Diet, which is divided into two chambers, the House of Representatives and the House of

Councillors. The civil service also has powers, and controls many aspects of business. The Liberal Democratic Party (LDP) has held power for most of the post-World War II period. In later years of its rule, it has been unable to obtain sufficient support to implement the economic changes that were considered necessary to reverse the recession of the late 90s and early 21st century. It currently holds power by way of a coalition with the Komeito Party. The main opposition is the Democratic Party.

Japan also has an emperor, this hierarchy of power emerging during the Meiji era in 1868. After the Second World War, however, this role was reduced to that of a constitutional monarch. Emperor Akihito currently holds this position, having assumed office in 1989 following the death of his long-serving father, Hirohito, who took office in 1926.

Religious, cultural and historical influences

Over the centuries, Japan has been exposed to the Chinese ways of Taoism and Confucianism. However, significant influence has also been brought to bear by the ways of Zen Buddhism, and Japan's home grown belief, Shinto.

Ethnic boundaries

In Japan, Zen and Shinto are almost complementary in their beliefs. While Buddhism concerns the afterlife, Shinto is oriented towards one's current existence. The principles of these, coupled with underlying Confucian beliefs, have created a single culture with a unique set of values, espousing the need to show great respect and politeness, particularly to senior and influential people.

Zen and Buddhism

Buddhism appeared in 552 AD, when King Paechke of Korea sent a Buddha image and scriptures to Japan. Since then the religion has undergone many transformations, such that its traditional form is now only one of many sects of Zen. There are now eight main Buddhist sects, with 13 smaller subgroups.

Zen is a corruption of the Buddhist word *dhyana* meaning "meditation". Through meditation (*zazen*), believers aim to achieve enlightenment.

Shinto

Shinto is a religion that is confined to Japan, and has origins going back to agrarian times before the birth of Christ. During the 19th century, under the auspices of the ruling emperor, it achieved recognition as a state religion. This was later rescinded after the Second World War.

Unlike many other religions, Shinto strives for favourable outcomes to auspicious occasions in family life on earth. This is accomplished by worshipping certain deities or *kami*, which assume a wide range of physical forms. Until the Second World War, emperors were designated *kami*, but after the war it was officially declared that no living person could be *kami*.

Historical Influences

There are no Japanese historical records prior to 600 AD. The only information available can be found in Chinese records. These, together with analyses of archaeological remains, suggest that before the birth of Christ there was a Polynesian and south-east Asian presence in the country.

Civil war broke out between 1156 and 1160, followed by periods of inept and corrupt administration. A military group known as the Genji assumed power in 1185, culminating in the first military-style government, or Shogun.

Following further periods of civil war, between 1603 and 1827, Leader Tokugawa ("The Edo") established a military (Bakufu) government in Tokyo and subsequently isolated Japan from the outside world. Civilian life was strictly regulated and Christianity suppressed. This so-called Edo period shaped the class distinction that is found in both business and society today.

In 1868, following further infighting, the Edo was replaced by Emperor Meiji, who revolutionised Japan from an isolated agricultural nation into a powerful industrialised country, with a modern navy and army – "The Meiji Restoration". In a quest for raw materials to sustain its industrial growth, Japan invaded China, Taiwan and Korea.

During the Second World War Japan invaded most south-east Asian countries, committing a large number of atrocities – the Rape of Nanking in China, the Death Railway in Thailand and the occupation of Singapore being the most notorious. At the end of the war, following the destruction of Hiroshima and Nagasaki, Japan rebuilt its nation to become the second largest economy in the world.

Social and business values

Today, the combined effects of Shinto, Buddhism and Confucianism dominate Japanese behaviour. Elders and seniors command great respect. Although in the Shinto faith living people cannot be designated *kami*, key decision makers, clients and customers may subconsciously be considered as such and treated as "gods" in their own right.

Japanese life is more formal and structured than that of other Asian groups, with greater emphasis on status in society and seniority in business. Japanese demeanour is reserved and respectful, with little room for spontaneity. Even when verbal disagreements occur, these tend to be conducted in a quiet manner, without loud outbursts. The working environment also tends to be highly structured, based on adherence to rules and regulations. A welcome sign once seen at the immigration counter at Tokyo's Narita airport is a stark reminder of this – "Welcome to Japan, but please obey the rules".

The policies of the Edo period of the 19th century have contributed to the ways of business in Japan today. During these times a class status was established, strict laws imposed and Japan sealed off from the influences of the rest of the world. Executives of western multinational companies are often frustrated when they find that their offices in Japan remain stubbornly isolated as non-conforming outposts, loyal to the local ways and unyielding to global corporate policies. The Edo class status still exists today and plays an important role in how business dealings are executed. In Japan, business stakeholders are valued differently from those in the West, as shown in the table below:

	West	**Japan**
Most important	Shareholder	Customer
Middle ranked	Customer	Employee
Least important	Employee	Shareholder

Customer-related issues are attended to promptly and efficiently, which is why service levels in Japan are among the highest in the world and why Japanese customers are so demanding. When competing in Japan, western companies should be aware of this trait and be prepared to improve their standards of service.

Japanese companies maintain a hierarchy of upper and middle management, similar to that found in western companies. However, in Japan, the higher echelons of seniority command far more reverence and respect from subordinates. The status levels are as follows:

>   *kaicho* (chairman)
>   *shacho* (president)
>   *jomu* (executive director)
>   *bucho* (departmental manager)
>   *kacho* (section manager)
>   *kakaricho* (supervisor)

Any level below *bucho* is deemed to be of a low status and is expected to "bow down" to more senior levels. Unfortunately, Japanese interpret many western middle-management titles as having lower status than their designations warrant. Sales-related functions are not highly regarded, as during the Edo era, merchants (equivalent to sales people of today) were deemed to have a low position in society. Age is also considered an important factor in determining an employee's level of seniority. It is unlikely that an older person will be found reporting to a younger manager.

Business in Japan is constructed around agreed frameworks which take time to establish but, once in place, form the basis of lasting future commitments. Japanese businessmen will go to great lengths to understand the management and decision-making structures of western organisations, leveraging these as much as possible.

The Japanese term for foreigners is *gaijin* ("outsider person"). In accordance with the Asian manner of taking time to develop relationships with foreigners, the Japanese can take this to extremes. It can take years to realise a first business transaction; quick breakthroughs should not be expected.

During their upbringing, Japanese women are taught to be subordinate to men and to care for and spoil their spouses. The Japanese word for wife (*okusan*) literally means "interior individual", implying that once they marry, a woman's place should be in the home. Western women with outgoing personalities should be prepared to assume a more subdued demeanour and expect not to always be afforded the usual courtesies that men enjoy. For instance, the normal custom of offering an important guest the seat of honour in a meeting room or restaurant may not always be applied to senior female executives.

In Japan, most working women perform junior secretarial and administrative duties, and are known as the "OL" the acronym for "office lady". The dominance of men in Japanese business is demonstrated by the fact that in 2004, women held only 2.7% of managerial positions in Japanese companies. Older Japanese may assume that a female member of a western business team is an OL, unless clear signals are given to the contrary. Thus a senior woman executive should demonstrate her status by following the protocols reserved for people of importance.

Fortunately, in modern Japan, as women are now treated with more equality western businesswomen should be shown the same level of respect as their male counterparts.

Local customs and etiquette

Special beliefs

Western visitors to Japan should be aware of the following special beliefs:

- The number "four" is considered very unlucky, as it is associated with death. Some buildings use different labels to depict the fourth floor. The number "nine" is also considered unlucky.
- In the Shinto way, Japanese pay special attention to ensuring favourable outcomes during life on earth.
- Black and white are not suitable colours, as they are used at funerals.
- Smiling can be seen as a sign of nervousness or embarrassment, rather than happiness.
- New Year's Day (1 January) is considered more important than Christmas, which is hardly celebrated at all. Japanese companies work on 25 December.
- Courtesy, respect, honour and patience are important traits.
- The practice of bowing is used in greeting, departing, expressing gratitude and apologising.
- An apology for any transgression, no matter how small, is seen as an act of extreme humility, far more so than in western countries.

Etiquette

When interacting with Japanese people **don't**:

- Admire objects possessed by others, as the owner may feel obliged to give the object to you!
- Use colloquialisms or jokes, as these will probably not be understood.
- Initiate discussions about Japanese atrocities committed over the last century.
- Pat someone on the back, or put an arm around the shoulders of another.
- Practise male-female shows of affection in public.

- Point your feet at anyone when seated on the floor, or when seated on a chair with your legs crossed.
- Use the American "OK" sign (thumb and forefinger curled in an "O"). This designates money.
- Use expansive arm movements or aggressive facial expressions.
- Point with the forefinger; rather use the open palm of the hand.
- Use a crooked index finger to beckon someone; rather use the standard Asian method of flapping your hand, palm down.
- Blow your nose loudly in public, as this is considered bad manners.
- Use a tissue or linen handkerchief when blowing the nose, and thereafter put it back in your pocket. Rather use a tissue and throw it away when you are finished. The Japanese view keeping a mucous-filled tissue or handkerchief as being highly unsanitary.
- Enter an occupied meeting room without first knocking on the door. This applies even when returning to the room after a short absence.

Preparation and awareness

Appointment scheduling

When establishing contact with a Japanese company for the first time, it is preferable, even in today's world of e-mail, to do this on a personal basis by telephone. Initial contact may result in a request for the caller to forward your company's background information. A company organogram should also be included. For first appointments, senior executives may be requested to submit their résumé in advance. The résumé need only be a brief half-page summary, clarifying their position in the organisation, educational background and personal or sporting interests.

There are three holiday periods during the year, and at these times it is not advisable to travel to Japan:

- New Year (28 December – 5 January): Most companies are closed at this time, so that employees can visit Shinto shrines to pray for a prosperous New Year ahead.
- Golden Week (29 April – 5 May): As there are four different public holidays in this short space of time, most Japanese take the entire week off for vacation or to visit relatives in remote parts of the country.
- *Obon* Season (mid August): Although not listed as a public holiday, mid August is the Obon season when all Japanese travel home to visit the graves of their ancestors.

Apart from the fact that business people might not be available during these times, travelling around Japan will be difficult because of huge crowds, particularly at airports. When planning an itinerary, plenty of time should be allowed to reach appointments in big cities. Japanese expect their visitors to be punctual.

Finding addresses in Japanese cities is challenging, in that the names and numbers of buildings are not always be displayed in English. Many streets have no names at all, and locating the street number of a building can be difficult. Addresses in Tokyo are designated by small districts called *chomes*, which are usually only a few blocks in area. Each building in a *chome* is assigned a one- or two-digit number, separated by a hyphen. To complicate matters further, up until 1955, building numbers were assigned in chronological order of construction, instead of location. Even taxi drivers struggle to find an exact address, despite circulating within the correct *chome*.

Gifts

Gifts are a significant part of Japanese life, and are presented as a sign of respect, particularly at first meetings. December and the July/August period are good times of the year for giving gifts, as these are normally offered with thanks for past support.

Appearance and presentation of gifts is extremely important, therefore much attention should be paid to the wrapping. Gift items can be curio articles from a home country, or items of food. An expensive and beautifully packaged food item is presented as a sign of respect. For example, perfectly spherical and cubic watermelons, specifically cultivated for sale as gift items, sell in the grocery sections of Tokyo department stores for US$60 each!

The following guidelines apply when choosing gifts:

- Gifts that contain a set of four of the same item should be avoided. Four is an unlucky number.
- Gifts should not be wrapped in black or white paper, as these colours are associated with funerals. White ribbons should not be used.
- White flowers, lilies, camellias, cyclamen or lotus blossoms should be avoided, as they are used at funerals. Chrysanthemums should also be avoided, as these are displayed in the emperor's royal crest.
- It is considered bad luck to give someone a potted plant if they are ill at home or in hospital. This draws an analogy that as the plant is rooted in soil, so will the recipient remain "rooted" in their sickbed.

As most Japanese are avid golfers, golf balls and miscellaneous golfing accessories will always be well received. It is quite acceptable to have golfing items branded with a company logo. Gifts are generally exchanged at the end of a meeting and should be handed over using both hands, and while bowing slightly.

Dress code

Business attire in Japan is formal and conservative. For men, a medium-to-dark suit and conservative tie is acceptable, and for women, suits with a skirt or trousers. As June, July and August can be unbearably humid, light linen attire is recommended. During the summer months, there has been a recent trend towards reducing energy costs by limiting the operating levels of air conditioners. To compensate, executives are permitted to wear open-neck short-sleeved shirts, instead of a jacket and tie.

As formal meals in Japanese restaurants often entail sitting on the floor, it is advisable to wear clothes that will facilitate getting up and down easily. Tall women should avoid wearing high heels so as not to dwarf Japanese men. Before entering Japanese restaurants, temples and some office or factory sites, shoes may have to be removed and placed at the entrance. It is therefore advisable to wear slip-off shoes rather than lace-up or strap-fastening footwear.

One notable accessory that should be carried is a handkerchief, for drying your hands. Many restrooms in public places or office buildings are not equipped with hand-drying facilities.

Both men and women should avoid using strong-smelling fragrances, as the Japanese do not appreciate these and can find them offensive.

Name cards

It will be necessary to pack plenty of name cards (*meishi*), as these are an essential part of business life in Japan. It is preferable that details be printed in Japanese on one side and in English on the other. People in a sales, marketing or business-development role should consider upgrading their western title. As junior (*kacho*) sales and marketing staff in Japan are treated with little respect, increasing the amount of *bucho* in a title elevates status, thus commanding more recognition. For instance, an advantage can be gained by changing the western title "marketing manager" to "general manager, marketing".

Meeting formalities

Names and forms of address

Japanese names comprise two words, the first being a given name and the second a family name. In keeping with the norms of politeness and formality, the correct form of address should be used when addressing men and women. When addressing or referring to a person, it is essential to use their family name and suffix it with *san*, the Japanese equivalent of Mr, Mrs or Miss. Thus the man Toshio Akita will be called "Akita-san" and the lady Mitsue Tanaka will be called "Tanaka-san", regardless of her marital status. A married woman assumes her husband's family name. Japanese businessmen also suffix company names with *san* when speaking among themselves.

It is unusual for a foreigner to use a Japanese person's given name, and only after a long and trusting relationship has developed will there be a chance that this might happen. Once a relationship has been established, a Japanese person may address a westerner by his or her given name, suffixed by *san*. This should not be construed as a signal that the westerner should do likewise. Unless specifically requested to do so, westerners should always continue to address a Japanese person by their family name.

Meeting and greeting

A greeting unique to Japan is the act of bowing (*ojiga*). Bowing is performed for many reasons, not only when meeting and departing, but also for apologising and expressing gratitude. It is a way of showing respect without having to engage direct eye contact. A deeper and longer bow is used for acknowledging older or more senior people. When men bow, their hands should be at their sides and in the case of women, the arms should be down and the hands clasped together in front of the body.

In order to make westerners feel more comfortable, the Japanese will shake hands and dispense with the bowing process. In this case, a light grip and brief handshake will suffice. A slight bow at the time of shaking hands, or immediately afterwards, is recommended.

The next important stage of the introduction process is the exchange of name cards, *meishi*. The presentation of *meishi* is one part of an elaborate and somewhat formal process of introduction. The visitor should be the first to offer his/her card. Similarly, a supplier should be the first to present his card to a customer. The card should be held with the index finger and thumb of both hands (as in the Chinese custom), then, as it is handed over, the left hand should be released and the card passed over with the right hand. The left hand is thus freed to receive the other person's card. Upon receiving a card, it should be glanced at intently and the owner's name pronounced. In Japan, *meishi* are deemed an extension of the owner, and should therefore be treated with extra care and respect. Bending, fiddling with or mutilating *meishi* in any way is highly disrespectful, although it is acceptable to write on them. They should never be placed in a back trouser pocket.

Preliminaries

In most big Japanese companies, a receptionist will show visitors to an empty meeting room. The hosts will enter the room shortly afterwards, with senior members of the delegation entering first.

Meeting rooms in Japan can be the normal western style, with a large table and chairs. For more important guests though, *osetsu*, a lounge setting with sofas and armchairs may be provided. When seated in the armchairs, your legs should not be crossed such that the foot of the crossed leg is pointing at anyone. It is preferable to keep both feet on the ground.

For company introductions, it is recommended that visitors present plenty of information depicting their company background. If overhead screen presentations are planned, it is advisable to notify the Japanese host in advance, so that a suitable meeting room can be allocated. As meetings arranged in *osetsu* do not facilitate use of audio-visual facilities, it is advisable to bring hard copies of electronic presentations.

As is the case elsewhere in Asia, the guest's seat of honour will be facing the door. The most senior person should sit in the middle. There are two exceptions to this:

- If there is a pleasing view out of a window, guests may be seated so that they can enjoy the view.
- Some rooms may have a small elevated alcove (*tokonami*), in which case the seats for the highest-ranking guests will be below the *tokonami*.

Smokers will be glad to know that in Japan smoking is permitted in office buildings and meeting rooms. For non-smokers this can be most unpleasant, particularly during stressful meetings – Japanese are known to chain-smoke when stressed.

Once a meeting has terminated, Japanese hosts escort departing guests from the office to the lift lobby. At this time, a departing bow or handshake will take place.

The most junior person of the visiting group should enter the lift first and stand at the back. Just before the lift doors close, it is normal for the hosts to bow again and for the group in the lift to reciprocate. Westerners should also adopt this practice when hosting Japanese visitors.

Negotiation etiquette

Most negotiations with large corporations are conducted in English, as at least one of the Japanese team will be able to interpret for the others. When dealing with smaller companies or in rural areas of Japan, an external interpreter may be required. Pidgin English should be avoided, as this may be perceived as insulting.

Meetings in Japan are usually conducted in a formal manner with little opportunity for humour. Laughter is usually used to hide embarrassment.

During initial meetings, Japanese may spend a considerable amount of time asking questions about one's home country, personal situation and general company background. They should be permitted to take the lead with regard to steering the conversation towards business-related matters.

Tolerance should be exercised when Japanese talk among themselves in their own language. Some of the group members may not understand English very well and therefore their interpreter will be required to explain issues. On account of this, meetings may take longer than expected.

Japanese people have difficulty in responding to questions phrased as double negatives. For example, the question "Don't you think it will be a good idea?" will receive a "No" reply if they think it is a good idea. The question should rather be phrased "Is this a good idea?" A vague reply may also arise when a question containing an "or" option is used. For example, when asking what to wear for an occasion, the question "Should I dress formally or casually?" will result in a "Yes" answer. The question should rather be phrased "Should I dress formally?"

One important feature of business life in Japan is *tatemae*. This is the subtle use of words to soften bad news, avoid conflict or flatter. Although it could be argued that in one form or another *tatemae* is practised in many countries, the Japanese are true masters. *Tatemae* is therefore used to avoid saying "No" in a direct manner, so as to prevent loss of face to themselves and/or the receiver of the negative news. Even saying "This will be difficult" is problematic for them, in that this response may still be too direct. Thus phrases such as "We'll think about it", "Let us see", "Perhaps", or "We'll consider it" may be heard. These convey far stronger negative meanings in Japan than they do in western environments.

Western negotiators should apply similar indirect phrases when responding in the negative, so as to avoid loss of face to the Japanese party.

Foreigners should not be misled by the word *hai* that is frequently used in Japan. *Hai* means "Yes, I hear you" or "I understand you", but does not necessarily mean, "Yes, I agree with you". Where there is complete agreement, a more affirmative answer would be forthcoming.

Obtaining a signature on a written agreement can be an extremely lengthy and frustrating experience, particularly if the Japanese legal department is not well versed in English. Provided company policy permits, and depending on the nature of the commercial circumstance, it is sometimes better to use a simple one or two page letter. The Japanese believe that once a framework agreement has been established, it should be honoured in full. For this reason many "contracts" in Japan are concluded on the basis of a verbal understanding.

Meals and entertainment

Invitations

On most work days Japanese employees do not return home for dinner after work and frequently eat out at a restaurant. Visitors should therefore be prepared for an after-hours invitation. Evening entertainment usually consists of dinner, followed by a visit to a hostess or *Karaoke* bar. Business entertainment is seldom done at home, as most Japanese homes are too small and too far away for this to be practical.

Food and drink

Food presentation is extremely important in Japan. Japanese dishes are always arranged elegantly, especially the raw fish dishes of sashimi and sushi. These are found on most menus in Japan. Of the two, sashimi is more challenging for the western palate, as it is nothing more than sliced raw fish: tuna, yellowtail, salmon and octopus being the most common. Sushi is similar, but comprises smaller pieces of raw fish on blocks of sticky rice, as well as cylindrical *maki*, which are vegetables or fish rolled in rice and wrapped in seaweed (*nori*). Sushi is prepared from a wide range of fish, eel (*unagi*), prawns (*ebi*), crab (*gani*), salmon roe (*ikura*) and sea urchin roe (*uni*). *Uni* is a delicacy among the Japanese, but foreigners will find it an "acquired taste" and should consume it with caution, as it has a distinctly sharp and strong flavour. The key to eating raw fish is that provided it is freshly prepared, there should be no offensive fishy smell or taste. To this end, most sushi bars in Japan use only the freshest fish, which is prepared immediately prior to eating. Both sashimi and sushi are eaten with soy sauce and a green spicy radish paste called *wasabi*. It is claimed that *wasabi* also acts as a "disinfectant" for the raw fish. *Wasabi* has a severe lachrymatory effect on the nasal passages, and should thus be used in limited quantities. It is usually mixed into a small bowl of soy sauce next to each diner's plate, and the fish piece or sushi portion dipped into it. True gourmets maintain that the soy sauce and *wasabi* should not be mixed beforehand, with the *wasabi* being added to the morsel after it has been dipped in the sauce.

Most other forms of Japanese food are served cooked and are very tasty, such as:
- *Sukiyaki*: Vegetables and meat are boiled in water in a heated pot at the table, and then removed from the water and dipped in a raw egg before being eaten. The morsel of food is usually hot enough to cook the egg that coats it.
- *Soba*: Noodles made of wheat which are served cold, and usually immersed in a bowl of light soy sauce – it is considered polite to slurp these while sucking them into the mouth, with the aid of chopsticks.

- *Teppanyaki*: Similar to a stir-fry of chicken, beef or prawns on a hot plate. A good "safe" meal.
- *Shabu Shabu*: Slices of Kobe beef and vegetables cooked in boiling water at the table, and dipped in either a sesame seed or soy sauce.
- *Tempura*: Prawns and vegetables deep-fried in batter.
- *Tonkatsu*: Pork fillet, battered and deep-fried, usually eaten with coleslaw and *daicon* radish.
- *Teriyaki*: Barbecued meat with sweet soy sauce.
- *Yakitori*: Small chicken kebabs.

Japanese meals are eaten with chopsticks, which differ from the Chinese variety in that they are shorter and more pointed at the ends. In some ways they are easier to use, except when picking up very small pieces such as grains of rice.

The Japanese are great drinkers, and beer is usually served at both lunch and dinner. In most cases, beer will be served in large quart bottles and poured into small glasses.

At dinner, after the first few rounds of beer, *sake* ("pure wine") is ordered. This is fermented rice mash, containing about 17% alcohol. It is consumed from small glasses, and can be served hot or cold. As *sake* contains a number of hangover-producing impurities, it is recommended that intake of this is carefully regulated. Hot *sake* finds its roots in the early days, before the advent of advanced purification techniques. It was found that pre-heating it just prior to consumption expelled any residual odour of mildew and soil. Today, the custom has been retained as it is claimed that hot *sake* is a better drinking experience, through which pleasant aromas are enjoyed. A stronger version of *sake*, *shochu*, distilled from rice, wheat and potatoes and containing 25 to 35% alcohol, may also be ordered. In spite of its higher alcohol content, *shochu* is not as hangover-inducing as *sake*, having been through a more rigorous distillation process.

Table etiquette

For business dinners, a separate room in a restaurant may be hired. The general rule regarding the seat of honour applies – the important guest sits facing the door, to the right of the most senior host. The Japanese meal table is usually rectangular and in formal situations guests sit on the floor, at a low table. While sitting on the floor, the feet should be tucked behind and not pointing at other diners. Foreigners suffering from back, knee or hip problems may find sitting on the floor for lengthy periods uncomfortable. In this instance, the nature of any such problem should be explained to the host well in advance, so that alternate seating arrangements can be found. To overcome such difficulties, the seating format of *hori gotatsu* can be suggested. In this format, diners still sit on the floor with their legs placed under the table in a sunken well, but use a legless chair (*zaisu*) for back support.

Prior to entering a dining area, guests are required to remove their shoes and walk around in stockinged feet. If there is a need to visit the restroom, a pair of slippers is provided for walking to and from the toilet. If there happens to be another pair of slippers outside the toilet door, these should be substituted and used to enter the toilet.

Japanese hosts order the meal and guests should not endeavour to order for themselves. Either individual appetisers or a shared dish, usually containing various forms of sashimi and sushi, will be served. Guests should not begin eating until the host has started. Main dishes are usually served as individual portions. Contrary to the custom in the West, women may not always be served first.

The most common soup found in Japan is *miso*, a tasty consommé made from fermented soya bean paste and tasting similar to that of yeast extract. It is consumed by removing the lid of the bowl and drinking from it, without using a spoon. Other ingredients found in the soup, such as small cubes of tofu, clams or seaweed, are eaten with chopsticks.

Rice is served either at the end or during a meal and is usually the sticky variety, which is easy to consume with pointed Japanese chopsticks.

Green tea is served near the end of a meal. Dessert is usually fruit or green-tea ice cream, which can be quite refreshing but is an acquired taste for some!

Table etiquette dictates that:

- Eating should not commence until the most senior person at the table has begun.
- Chopsticks should not be stuck into the rice bowl so that they stand up – this is only done at funerals.
- The rice bowl should not be lifted up to the mouth as is practised in China.
- Pointing or gesticulating with chopsticks should be avoided.
- When picking up a piece of food to pass on to someone else, your chopsticks should be reversed so that the square top-end is used to grip the morsel.
- The mouth should be covered with a hand, while using a toothpick.
- Slurping while drinking soup or eating noodles is considered polite, and is expected!

A golden rule in drinking with Japanese is that on no account should drinkers pour alcohol for themselves. Good etiquette dictates that someone else at the table should pour for another. It is customary for the recipient to give a nod of appreciation and lift the glass with both hands during the pouring process. When the glass has been filled, the receiver should pick up the bottle and pour for anyone else nearby whose glass is in need of a refill. While pouring, both hands should be used to support the bottle. Once the beverage has been poured, it is customary to wait for the host to begin drinking. The Japanese version of "bottoms up" is *kanpai*. Italians should be forewarned that the Italian word for cheers, *chin-chin*, is highly inappropriate as in Japanese this is a vulgar word.

Japanese drinking etiquette, especially in formal environments, dictates that women should observe the feminine technique of raising the glass with the one hand, supporting the bottom with the other and bending the head lightly forward to take a sip. Only men are permitted to take mouthfuls!

It is normal procedure for the host to pay for a meal. Settlement is not always done in the western manner, where the bill is brought to the table. This transaction is normally delegated to a more junior person in the host party. It is customary for the payer to leave the table and settle the bill at the front desk, while everyone else finishes the meal.

Evening entertainment

In Japan, further entertainment is usually offered after dinner. Although during working hours Japanese maintain a formal and reserved demeanour, this changes as the evening progresses. It is time for everyone to relax and become more open, and for subordinates to assume a more equal status with their superiors. As this is an excellent opportunity for relationship-building between businessmen of different cultures, any such invitation should readily be accepted. To decline an invitation would cause loss of face to the host.

In most cases, after-dinner entertainment will take the form of a visit to a hostess bar. These are small salons arranged in a formal manner to permit small groups of men to drink together, served by hostesses who will sit and make polite conversation. Where foreigners are included, more often than not there will be a language barrier, so conversation will be nothing more than small talk. Female colleagues will probably not be invited to this form of entertainment, although visiting western businesswomen forming part of a male delegation may be included, being granted male status for the occasion! At bars with *karaoke* facilities guests will be expected to sing.

In Tokyo, upmarket and very expensive nightclubs are to be found in the exclusive shopping district of Ginza, while more daring and less-refined entertainment is provided in the infamous Roppongi district. Here, the wide range of imaginative nightclubs and entertainment spots are targeted mainly at the younger set.

Another option, mainly for drinking, is a visit to an *Izakaya* ("sit and drink") that specialises in serving various kinds of *sake* and *shochu*. Those with a weak drinking constitution should take care – as the name implies, one is expected to drink for an extended period.

Regardless of the type of entertainment, the evening will usually end at around 11 pm as most Japanese have long train journeys back home. Sometimes at the end of a meal or entertainment session, a Japanese host may comment on an important business matter as a parting shot. Usually, such profound remarks are of significance and should be carefully noted.

7 Korea

The country name South Korea, also referred to as "The Republic of Korea", is distinct from its northern neighbour the "Democratic Peoples' Republic of Korea" (DPRK). Both countries form the Korean peninsula, which extends south from northern China. There are over 2 000 small islands distributed around the main South Korean peninsula.

In the early part of Korea's history, under a dynasty system, a large portion of the Korean peninsula extended into China. Korean culture, therefore, has extensive Confucian origins. During the 20th century, Japan occupied Korea for 35 years, leaving residual elements of Japanese culture. There has also been an infiltration of American ways among younger members of the population, owing to an American military presence in the country. For the most part though the country has one homogeneous culture, with deep-rooted Korean customs still ingrained in the majority of the population.

Country background

Population
The population of Korea is 48 million.

Ethnicity and religion
The majority (99.9%) of the population is ethnic Korean. There is a small group of Chinese people. Only half of the population claim to follow any religion, including Christianity (21%), *Mahayana* Buddhism (24%), and spirit worship (Shamanism).

Language and script
The Korean language dates back to before the birth of Christ. The written form was originally based on Chinese characters. During the 15th century, a new written language known as *Hungeul* was introduced. It comprises 24 letters (10 vowels and 14 consonants). The alphabet is phonetic and the spoken form, *Hunkuk Mal,* is not tonal. The pronunciation of the English translation of Korean words is relatively straightforward, although *Hungeul* does not have "F" or "Z" sounds. When Korean words are translated into English, some consonants are interchangeable. This is because in 2002, the Korean government adopted a new Romanised system, which resulted in a change of consonants and vowel combinations, as given below:

Before 2002	After 2002
P	B
T	D
K	G
CH	J
O	EO
U	EU

The names of Korean places can therefore be spelt differently, causing confusion as to whether the same place is being referenced. Examples of this are Pusan and Busan (both naming the same port located on the southern tip of the Korean peninsula), Taejon and Daejon (a town situated in the middle of the country) and Kwangju and Gwangju, also the name of a town. The resort island of Jeju was previously called Cheju. The town Kyongju is spelled Gyeongju under the new system.

Some forms of Chinese writing (*Hanmun*) also remain, and can be seen in newspapers and other publications. Koreans consider the ability to read Chinese a sign of good breeding, education and status.

Regional structures

Korea is divided into nine provinces, one special city (being the capital Seoul) and the six metropolitan cities of Busan, Daegu, Incheon, Gwangju, Daejon and Ulsan.

Political environment

Korea is a multiparty republic, governed by a democratically elected president who oversees the State Council of Ministers (the Cabinet). There is also a National Assembly of 273 members that is elected every four years. The president is elected through democratic elections held every five years. The ruling party is the URI Party, with the Grand National Party forming the opposition.

Religious, cultural and historical influences

Korea is often mistaken as being primarily Buddhist, yet only a quarter of the population follow this religion. Christianity is the next largest religious group, a quarter of which is Catholic and the remainder Protestant. The many red crosses on top of church spires that light up the Seoul skyline at night are evidence of this large Christian following. Although in early times Confucianism was deemed a state religion, it has since changed to a code of ethics which still influences contemporary Korean ways.

Ethnic boundaries

As Korea is one of the strongest and most widely Confucian-based societies in Asia, its population can be regarded as having a single, unified culture.

Confucianism

The teachings of Confucius arrived in Korea from China, during the 4th century. The Joseon dynasty adopted Confucianism as a national ideology and established a class distinction between noble and lower classes, as well as a family system of moral and social codes. To this day, the head of a family exerts absolute control over the household and represents the family in worshipping ancestors. Filial piety is practised in most families, with great respect being shown to seniors and elders.

Buddhism

The kingdom of Paekche/Goguryeo in the south-west of Korea first adopted Buddhism in the 4th century. Buddhism appeared as the *Mahayana* or "greater vehicle" form, originating from China. It was later designated the national religion during the Goryeo dynasty. During the subsequent Joseon Dynasty, Confucianism superceded Buddhism and today Korea has one of the strictest Confucian societies in Asia. Despite this, Buddhism still maintains a significant presence in the country.

Christianity

Christianity appeared in Korea with the arrival of Catholic missionaries during the mid-19th century, when the country opened its doors to the West. During this time, however, Confucianism suppressed the development of Catholicism. It was only when Protestant missionaries arrived later in the century, that Christianity flourished.

Historical influences

Korea has a long history dating back to 2333 BC, when the ancient kingdom of Chosun ("land of the morning calm") was founded by a mythical figure called Tangun. At this time, North Korea was united with South Korea. The Chosun era lasted for 2 400 years, followed later by a period of Dynasties which lasted until 1910. Until 1882 Korea was isolated from the western world, when America became the first western nation to establish diplomatic relations with Korea.

In 1910 Japan seized control of Korea and retained this for 35 years, until the end of the Second World War. During the time of occupation, Korean culture was suppressed in favour of Japanese ways. Cities were renamed in Japanese and the populace ordered to assume Japanese names and to speak only Japanese. There is still a residual resentment of Japan by older Koreans, whose kin were subjected to such treatment.

When Japan was forced to surrender at the end of World War II, an agreement between the US and Russia resulted in Korea splitting at the 38th parallel into North and South. Shortly afterwards North Korea attacked South Korea, leading to the Korean War in which the US became embroiled.

In 1953, after much bloodshed, an armistice was declared and a 4 km wide and 250 km long Demilitarised Zone ("DMZ") established. The Democratic Peoples' Republic of Korea (DPRK) has remained isolated from the rest of the world, is strongly communist and is bent on military aggression towards its neighbours. A strong

American military presence has been retained in South Korea, with the result that the populace has adopted elements of "Americana".

After the War, a number of major industrial groups, or *chaebols*, emerged. Most of these are highly diversified conglomerates that began as family-owned businesses. Intense competition between the *chaebols* created rapid expansion and diversification across a broad range of industries, such as construction, electronics and chemicals. Today these form the backbone of the Korean economy. The biggest Korean *chaebols* are: Hyundai, Samsung, LG, SK, Hanjin, Daelim and Kia.

Social and business values

Like all Confucian-dominated societies, Koreans show respect for seniors and the elderly and recognise class distinctions. Possession of good qualifications is extremely important, bringing with it status and pride to the family unit. This also applies to the concept of *yangban*, where nobility, high-ranking scholars and military personnel are revered. For this reason, teachers and educators are highly respected in Korean society.

As much of Korea's modern history is military-based (Korea's strong military culture originates from its mid-20th century government), there is a "can do" attitude to getting things done.

As with most Asian cultures, Koreans respect the needs of a group and individualism is frowned upon. It is important that harmony is maintained at all times within a working group.

In family life, the husband is dominant and commands great respect from other members. For this reason, as in China, sons are highly valued. On marriage, the wife joins the husband's family. Women enjoy little status – for instance, it is customary for a Korean woman to open the door for a man and to allow him to proceed first! The status of women, however, is now improving. For example, the high divorce rate in Korea (now 40%, the fourth highest in the world) results primarily from women's actions against their errant husbands. The days when a woman was considered a possession of her husband are rapidly receding. For instance, in 2006, President Roh Moo-hyun proposed that Han Myeong-sook be nominated Korea's first female prime minister.

Korean business society is, however, still male-dominated and during business discussions western women are advised to assume a quiet and submissive demeanour. Senior women executives will have to demonstrate their status by following the etiquette protocols of the hierarchy, failing which they may be mistaken for junior support staff.

There are three principal mechanisms through which Koreans interact:

- *Ch'emyon*: an outward show of prestige, confidence and dignity, or having face.
- *Nunchi*: identification of a person's inner feelings without verbal cues.
- *Gibun*: an aura or life force.

Gibun is a complex and subtle subject and can best be defined as feeling happy by maintaining a high level of self-esteem. Loss of *ch'emyon* (or face) can have a negative effect on one's *gibun*. *Nunchi* is the ability of Koreans to determine another person's mood from their *ch'emyon,* and knowing how to react appropriately so as to restore lost *ch'emyon* and hence promote *gibun.* The subtlety with which these three important cultural elements are deployed among Koreans is beyond the comprehension of most westerners. In many cases, messages and feelings are conveyed through actions rather than verbal exchanges.

It is possible to elevate a Korean's *ch'emyon* and *gibun* in the way they are addressed, treated and respected. Conveyance of negative information can affect a person's *gibun,* and is normally done as indirectly as possible. Bad news may not be imparted early in the morning, for fear of spoiling the receiver's *gibun* for the remainder of the day. Care should be taken to avoid both direct and unintentional implied criticism of anything Korean. Koreans have a way of elevating *gibun* through tactful use of actions and indirect innuendoes – *nunchi.* A simple example is the question "Do you like Korean food?" This question may be asked not because the originator of the question is concerned about culinary tastes, but because he is anticipating a positive response that will inflate his *gibun.* It is recommended that a subtle positive answer be given, even if Korean food is disliked.

Networking plays a significant role in Korean business. Business deals may be concluded on the strength of a long-standing interpersonal relationship, rather than pure commercial terms. The manner in which networks are deployed can be extremely complex, involving a number of players. For example, companies wishing to sell their products to a Korean company may be instructed to use a particular agent nominated by a person of influence in that company. This agent may be a personal friend or ex-colleague of the decision-maker of the company. Regrettably, this practice is quite common in Korea, which creates a dilemma for western companies with high standards of integrity and governance.

As Confucian principles have considerable influence on Korean behaviour in business, it stands to reason that Korean companies have a structured hierarchy. It is always important to match the age and seniority of a western business delegation with that of the Korean side. Etiquette may be transgressed if a young, loud and outgoing person is tasked with meeting an older or more conservative Korean businessman.

Contrary to the ways of most other Asian cultures, Koreans are keen to get down to business matters as quickly as possible. When needs be they can be surprisingly forthright and direct. In sales situations, matters of price and terms are raised at an early stage and direct feedback is usually quite easy to obtain. Nonetheless, final decisions will still be referred back to a more senior person.

Notwithstanding the fact that Korean dealings may not always be straightforward, they do expect westerners to be honest and consistent in their approach to doing business. Koreans are reluctant to openly disagree and feel uncomfortable during confrontation.

Koreans, like Taiwanese are tough negotiators, especially when they are in a position of strength. Westerners should always be prepared to consider making at least two or three rounds of concessions, particularly on matters pertaining to price. The manner in which concessions are granted can have an impact on personal relationships. When negotiating from a position of strength, it is still advisable to give small concessions as a sign of willingness to build the relationship. When in a position of weakness, concessions should not be given quickly, but reluctantly, and with a purpose. Notwithstanding the finalisation of an agreement, Koreans may still seek further concessions, even though a clear business framework has been agreed.

Local customs and etiquette

Special beliefs

Western visitors to Korea should be aware of the following special beliefs:

- The number "four" is considered very unlucky, as it is associated with death. Some buildings do not label the fourth floor in lifts with a numeric "4". Instead, an "F" may be substituted. There are no significant lucky numbers, although older Koreans believe that the number three is lucky.
- Black and white are not considered cheerful or lucky colours, as they are used at funerals. At a Korean funeral, men wear black and women wear white. Most other colours are acceptable.
- Because of the relatively large number of Christian followers in Korea, Christmas and Easter are important times of the year.
- Courtesy, respect and honour are important aspects of daily life.
- Junior people are expected to show humility and respect to their seniors.
- The act of bowing is used when greeting, expressing gratitude and apologising, but is practised on a less formal basis than in Japan.
- It is common to see females holding hands in public. This is a display of kinship or close friendship.

Etiquette

When interacting with Koreans, **don't**:

- Criticise anything Korean, either directly or by implication. Regional biases exist between citizens of different towns, and a foreigner might be tested with "the OR question". A Korean may ask "Do you prefer Seoul or Daejon?" or "Do you prefer Japanese food or Korean food?" These questions are more than simple queries. They are intended to draw the unsuspecting foreigner to respond with a positive *ch'emyon* and a *gibun*-enhancing reply.
- Be surprised if a Korean asks how old you are – he is merely trying to establish relative levels of seniority to determine how much respect should be shown to you.
- Assume that when a Korean verbally expresses a large number, the amount is correct. Koreans deal in multiples of 10 000 and when translating into English, can mistakenly exclude or add a zero to the number. To avoid ambiguity, it is best to ask them to write down the figure.
- Declare that you are from a non-prestigious family background. Koreans respect academic and business achievements, and look down on practical work and labour.

- Laugh loudly – women should cover their mouths with their hands when laughing.
- Cross the legs, particularly in front of a more senior or elderly person. This applies to men only. It is acceptable for women to cross their legs.
- Practise the western habit of patting on the back or putting an arm around the shoulders of a Korean. This is considered extremely rude. Public displays of affection between members of the opposite sex should be avoided.
- Beckon or call out to a senior or elderly person. Rather approach them.
- Smoke in the presence of a more senior or elderly person.
- Interrupt a more senior or elderly person when they are talking, particularly during negotiations.
- Initiate discussion about a Korean's wife, or try to mention her by name.
- Blow the nose loudly. If this has to be done in public, do it quietly. The Asian custom of sniffing is considered more polite.
- Sneeze loudly. Sneezes should be muffled as much as possible.
- Write or present literature with triangles on it. Sharp corners imply disharmony.
- Write a person's name in red, as this implies that the person has died or is scheduled to die.
- Point with the forefinger; rather use the open palm of the hand.
- Be intolerant of the smaller personal body space of Koreans. Korea is one of the most densely populated Asian countries. As over 70% of the country is mountainous, the population is concentrated in the lower-lying urban areas. Queuing is not always practised, and pushing and shoving may be done without apology or concern.
- Promote Japan or anything Japanese in front of an elderly Korean. They still harbour a resentment of Japan, following its 35 years of oppressive occupation.

Preparation and awareness

Appointment scheduling

In keeping with the Korean business trait of networking, whereby personal contacts are leveraged as much as possible, initial approaches by fax or e-mail for a first-time appointment may not always be answered. As face-to-face personal contact is preferred, use of a Korean third party such as a representative from a local trade commission may achieve a more positive result. In many cases, the Korean contact may suggest the name of an "agent" through which business should be channelled.

Women should take special care to designate their gender when communicating in writing for the first time, otherwise it will automatically be assumed they are male. Similarly, if women are to be included in a visiting party of western men, the Korean party should be notified beforehand.

A senior member of a western team may elevate his status through Korean eyes by surrounding himself with subordinates, who should be seen to be attentive to his needs. This is in keeping with the Korean mentality of *yangban,* where nobility and high-ranking staff are highly respected.

There are two holiday periods in the year when it is not advisable to schedule appointments:

◻ *Seolnal:* the Lunar New Year (the equivalent of Chinese New Year). Koreans pronounce it as *"Seollal",* as they have difficulty pronouncing "n" after "l".

◻ *Chuseok:* which takes place during August or September. Most Koreans return to their home towns to visit relatives and pay respect to their ancestors.

Virtually the entire country closes over these periods. As both these holiday periods are lunar-based, they do not always occur on the same date each year.

When scheduling appointments in Seoul, remember that despite a fast and efficient underground rail system, traffic can become congested. Koreans are not afraid to cancel meetings at short notice, using the excuse that their boss has summoned them or they have to travel to an office in another location. This may happen regardless of how far a visitor has travelled to honour an appointment.

Foreigners travelling on their own may find it difficult to locate an address, particularly if the company is small or relatively unknown. Building and street names are not always clearly displayed in English and in some cases, streets do not have names. As in Japan, the western way of numbering street addresses does not apply in Korea. Addresses are based on wards (*gu*) and smaller subsections (*dong*), roughly the size of a large block. Each building is allocated a number within a *dong.* Seoul has twenty-five *gu* and hundreds of *dongs*! When travelling by taxi, it is advisable to have the destination address written down in *Hungeul* for the taxi driver, as few are proficient in English.

Although in bigger Korean corporations English is fairly well understood, in smaller organisations and in more remote areas it may be necessary to arrange for an interpreter. This person can also assist in locating addresses that are difficult to find. As Korea is a male-dominated society, a male rather than a female interpreter should be used.

Gifts

Gifts for Koreans should be selected such that the receiver's *gibun* will be elevated and they will feel honoured, but without feeling obliged to reciprocate. In Korean terms, giving a gift can also be seen as a way of apologising when asking for a favour. For instance, when seeking a major concession, a gift may be presented at the end of the meeting as an apology. Typical items might be a designer tie, a handkerchief, a pen or a bottle of expensive alcohol.

The following guidelines apply when choosing gifts:

◻ During the Lunar New Year and *Chuseok* holiday periods, gifts such as alcohol and fruit may be given.

◻ Gifts should not be wrapped in black or white paper, as these colours are associated with funerals.

◻ White flowers should only be given at funerals.

- Gifts that contain sets of four of the same item should not be given. Four is considered an unlucky number.
- Gifts of Japanese origin should be avoided, especially if they are designated for older Koreans.
- Koreans tend to present gift items sporting famous brand names – it would be worthwhile to follow this custom.

Gifts are generally exchanged at the end of a meeting. They should be handed over using the two-handed technique, together with a slight bow. Sometimes the gift may be refused, but this is merely a customary formality – the gift should be offered again, and possibly a third time, after which it should be accepted.

Dress code

Business attire in Korea is conservative and formal. Confucius once said: "Clothes distinguish a cultured man from a barbarian". Koreans take this to heart, and being mindful of their personal appearance tend to dress well and conservatively. For men, a medium-to-dark suit, a white long-sleeved shirt and a conservative tie are acceptable, and for women, a jacket and matching skirt. In the hot months of June to August, a short-sleeved shirt with a jacket and tie is permitted. As meals can be taken sitting on the floor in traditional Korean restaurants, it is advisable to wear clothes that will facilitate getting up and down off the floor easily. As shoes are removed for dining on the floor, it is advisable to wear slip-on shoes rather than lace-up or strap-fastening footwear.

Apart from their dress sense, Koreans are also fastidious about their grooming, and most executives maintain a clean-cut appearance.

Name cards

As most Koreans are able to understand English well, it is not necessary to have cards printed in Korean. As academic titles afford greater recognition in Korean business circles, university qualifications should be displayed on the card. This is essential for women, as they should aim to elevate their importance as much as possible.

Meeting formalities

Names and forms of address

To the uninitiated, Korean names can be confusing. Usually a Korean person's name is shown as three words, with the family name appearing first, followed by two given names. The second given name may be generational, similar to the Chinese custom. Sometimes, though, given names appear first, conforming to the western way.

There are several tips for identifying a Korean family name:

- There are only 286 family names in Korea. The following family names belong to more than half the population: Lee (or Rhi and Yi), Kim, Cho, Chong or Park (actually Pak, but spelt as such for easier English pronunciation).
- The two given names are usually hyphenated.

- When given names are shown first, there will usually be a comma separating the second given name from the family name.
- Given names may also be abbreviated to initials, which appear before the family name.
- Examples of the most common structure of Korean names are:
  Choung Sung-Ik ("Mr Choung")
  Jung-Lee, Kwan ("Ms Kwan")
  Y.B. Han ("Mr Han")
  (In each case the family name has been underlined.)

It is essential to correctly identify the family name, as there is a high degree of formality in the way Koreans address one another. It is vital that they should be called Mr or Ms {family name}, even after a long-standing relationship has been developed. First names should not be used by westerners. Where a person of seniority is being addressed (such as a senior director) by a more junior person, they may be called "director" {family name}. Although an older or more senior person may be permitted to call a more junior person by their given name, under no circumstances will a junior person be permitted to reciprocate – this is in keeping with the Confucian principle of respect for elders and seniority.

Korean women do not assume their husband's family name on marriage. Women are not normally addressed by name, as Koreans have their own unique way of referring to women. For example, a woman married to Mr Lee will be referred to as "wife of Mr Lee". Westerners will find it difficult to distinguish between male and female given names. Female members of a western delegation should always be referred to by their family name, preceded by Mrs or Ms.

Meeting and greeting

As in Japan, Koreans bow slightly when meeting one another, but the process is not as formal. The western handshake is commonly used in the business environment, particularly when greeting foreigners. In the Korean world, it is necessary to display both hands when shaking hands or passing over articles. This act is accomplished by using the palm of the left hand to support the underside of the right forearm, or via a double-handed handshake. A brief light handshake is all that is necessary, and a strong pumping action should be avoided. A slight bow can be given after the handshake. This traditional gesture demonstrates honour and respect. Another theory maintains that this technique is used to prove that a harmful weapon is not being concealed behind the back.Men should not initiate a handshake with a Korean woman, unless she offers her hand. If she does not, a slight bow will suffice. Similarly, western women will have to initiate a handshake with a Korean man, failing which a slight bow can be given.

Name cards are handed across with two hands or using the right hand only, with the right forearm supported by the palm of the left hand. A slight bow can be made when the card is presented.

Preliminaries

On entering a meeting room, senior members of a visiting delegation should enter first. Guests should wait for an invitation to be seated. The normal Asian etiquette of taking seats facing the door, with the most senior guest located in the middle of this group, applies. If one of the walls contains an ornament or picture (similar to a *tokonami,* as found in Japan) the most important guest may be invited to sit below this. If refreshments are offered, it is considered impolite to refuse them.

On completion of a meeting, hosts will usually escort visitors to the lift lobby and see them into the lift. Just before the lift doors close a slight bow may be given by the hosts, which should be reciprocated by those in the lift.

Negotiation etiquette

Koreans can be surprisingly direct and sometimes quite demanding during discussions. This can manifest itself in what may appear to be short-tempered and aggressive behaviour. During meetings with westerners, Koreans tend to dispense with time-wasting pleasantries and small talk. They may converse among themselves in Korean in a way that may appear aggressive, but to a large extent this is merely the way their language comes across to foreigners. When speaking, slow, clear and simple speech should be used. Pidgin English should be avoided, as this may be perceived as insulting. Reference to groups rather than individuals is extremely important in Korea and any attempt to exhibit individualism will be frowned upon. Therefore the words "we" and "our" rather than "I" and "my" are preferred.

Periods of silence during discussions are common – it is acceptable in the Korean world to take time to reflect before responding. Older or more senior people should not be interrupted while they are talking. While the technique may require a lot of practice, it is important to try to elevate Korean *ch'emyon* at various stages of the proceedings by making suitable indirect remarks of flattery. For example, the compliment "You are a very tough negotiator, Mr Kim", will be well received.

As with most other Asian cultures, Koreans will avoid face-losing responses by giving evasive answers. As Koreans consider continuous eye contact impolite, westerners should limit direct eye contact during business discussions. Westerners should not construe that a Korean is being devious when he does not look them in the eye.

Once a framework agreement has been established with Koreans, westerners should anticipate that they might propose substantial modifications in the future. In expectation of this, westerners should be prepared to be flexible.

Meals and entertainment

Invitations

As in most Asian cultures, development of interpersonal relationships is extremely important in Korea and is seen as integral to business. After-hours entertainment involving heavy drinking sessions is considered a necessary part of this process.

As networking and leveraging of long-standing personal relationships has such an important role in the local business environment, foreign businessmen should comply with this important facet of Korean business life. Being a male-dominated society, wives are not included in business-related functions. Invitations to dinner should be accepted, as it is considered impolite to refuse. After the meal there may be further invitations to go drinking.

Food and drink

Koreans like food that contains garlic and chilli. Almost every meal in Korea, including breakfast, will be dominated by *kimchi*. This is a spicy concoction of cabbage and radish that has been marinated in a mixture of chilli, garlic and other spices. For some this may be an acquired taste. Most Korean food is palatable to westerners, but it should be pointed out that Koreans are partial to eating dog, which is offered by restaurants specialising in this cuisine. Another dish to avoid is *cheong kuk jang*, an offensive-smelling soup of fermented soya beans.

There are fortunately several "safe" options for westerners to select, when asked which Korean dishes they prefer:

- *Bulgogi*: Also known as the Korean barbeque, is the most famous of the local dishes. Diners sit together around a charcoal brazier, upon which thinly cut slices of beef and cut ribs are barbequed. These tend to have a stronger taste than beef barbequed in the western way.
- *Kalbi*: Beef ribs that have been boiled or braised.
- *Man'doo*: Small Korean dumplings containing either pork, tofu or vegetables. Similar to the *dim sum* found in Hong Kong, and a good option at lunchtime.
- *T'ang* and *kuk*: Types of soup served in a large bowl, together with rice. These are meals in themselves.

Koreans consume a vast range of soups. It is common for cold noodles (*naeng myon*) or rice to be served at the end of a meal.

As Koreans are great drinkers, beer may be served in the business environment with both lunch and dinner. The local speciality, though, is *soju*, a potent rice wine liquor that resembles vodka, with an alcohol content of between 18 and 25%. As the many hangover-inducing impurities in *soju* are not removed through a proper distillation process, this form of alcohol should be consumed with care.

Table etiquette

Koreans enjoy partaking of meals while seated on the floor, against a low rectangular table (*bapsang*). This setting is often used for the Korean barbeque. If sitting on the floor for extended periods presents a problem, it is advisable to explain this to the host before a restaurant is selected, as some restaurants offer floor seating only. When sitting on the floor, men should sit cross-legged, while women sit with their legs to one side.

Koreans eat with chopsticks, but these differ from those found in China or Japan. They are unique to Korea, made of stainless steel, and are thinner and flatter than most other forms. Westerners who are not proficient with chopsticks will find these extremely difficult to use, as they tend to slip and slide over the fingers. A round spoon with a long handle will also be provided. The spoon is used for selecting food items from communal dishes and for drinking soup.

Kimchi is always served as a starter, and is also consumed throughout the meal. A meal usually consists of a main dish, accompanied by a large number of smaller side dishes of condiments (*panch'an*). Most dishes, including soup, are served at the same time and are eaten on a communal basis. Koreans have an amazing capacity to rapidly consume huge quantities of food. Foreigners may find it difficult to keep pace, as their ability to eat quickly may be hampered by their lack of proficiency with the Korean chopsticks. Towards the end of the meal, noodles or rice will be served. The rice may be mixed in with the sauce remnants of an earlier dish and then served into individual rice bowls.

As Koreans do not normally eat rich desserts, it is common for a few pieces of sliced fruit to be served at the end of a meal. This will be served on a communal plate from which diners help themselves.

Table etiquette dictates that:

◘ Guests should not begin eating a course until the most senior person at the table has begun.
◘ It is not polite to smoke in front of a senior person, at the dinner table.
◘ Chinese chopstick etiquette applies in Korea.
◘ Soup may be consumed with the spoon that is provided. Although sometimes practised, lifting the soup bowl to drink is not appropriate.
◘ It is not necessary to slurp noodles in the Japanese way in order to be polite, although noisy eating sounds are acceptable.
◘ The fingers should not be used for eating – chopsticks should be used at all times, even for eating cut fruit, unless dessert forks have been provided.
◘ When passing food plates or other items across the table, the right hand should be used, with the forearm supported by the left hand.
◘ Bones and crustacean shells are placed on the table, not on the food plate.
◘ Eating utensils should not be placed in a soup bowl, or on a plate, when not in use. They should simply be placed on the table.
◘ If it is necessary to blow your nose, this should not be done at the table, but rather in the toilet. It is, however, quite acceptable to sniff at the table!

In the Japanese way, small glasses are provided for drinking alcohol. The host will pour for guests, starting with the most senior guest. The receiver should lift his glass with both hands while pouring is taking place. While pouring beer, either both hands should hold the bottle, or if only one hand is being used, the other hand should be placed under the forearm of that being used to hold the bottle. Guests should not start drinking until the eldest or most senior host has started, or invited everyone to begin. When drinking *soju*, it is customary for a drinker to pass his glass to another person (usually someone of the same seniority), fill the glass, after which the receiver is expected to down it in one go. The receiver then reciprocates by passing his glass across and filling it for his "partner", who then downs the contents. This simple gesture is symbolic of friendship and bonding.

It is customary for the person who arranged the meal to pay. Sometimes arguments may be witnessed among Korean diners as to who should pay, but ultimately the host will settle the bill. Normal etiquette dictates that the bill may not be brought to the table and that the host pays at the front desk, just before leaving. Koreans do not linger once a meal is over, and depart almost immediately. After all, there is the next item on the entertainment menu, the drinking session!

Evening entertainment

Koreans are notorious for their after-dinner drinking sessions, used as a means of cementing relationships. Getting drunk together provides common ground from which to go forward, and normally such sessions can extend into the small hours of the morning. This tends to be a male-dominated pastime, and for this reason women will not be invited. Korean society frowns on females drinking alcohol in public, and when Koreans entertain at home, the wives will normally leave their husbands and guests to drink together. Hence western women are advised to excuse themselves after dinner, to allow their male associates to attend the drinking session unencumbered.

Two popular areas for evening entertainment in the capital, Seoul, are Myungdog, a restaurant and bar area that buzzes at night, and Itaewon, famous for its restaurants and extensive range of bargain shops.

The normal venue for drinking is a hostess bar (*room salon*), similar to those found in Japan. Drinks are served by glamorous waitresses, whose function it is to sit and converse with customers. Side snacks (*anju*) of dried fish, nuts and fruit will also be served. Western guests may encounter a language barrier as not many hostesses are able to speak English.

Given the Korean concept of group bonding, it is preferable that the entire group gets drunk together. It is therefore good manners to drink everything that is offered by the host, even to the point of drunkenness. Care should be exercised regarding the type of alcohol imbibed, as in most cases this will be *soju*, whiskey or both!

Any westerner wishing to limit his consumption of alcohol can plead that a medical condition prevents excessive alcohol intake. Alternatively, a hostess can be encouraged to water down an alcoholic drink!

Koreans may at the end of a meal or entertainment session comment on an important business matter as a parting shot. Usually such remarks are of significance, and should be carefully noted.

8 Indonesia

Indonesia is a vast country with a wide range of different ethnic tribes distributed over more than 13 000 islands, the largest being Sumatra, Java, Sulawesi and Kalimantan. Its name is derived from the Greek words "Indos" meaning Indian, and "nesos" meaning islands. It is the most populous nation in south-east Asia, having the fourth largest population in the world, and is the world's largest archipelago. During the nineties Indonesia was one of the fastest-growing countries in Asia, contributing significantly to regional growth. It has subsequently suffered from economic mismanagement and intertribal conflicts.

Although Indonesia is predominantly Muslim, there is a small Chinese population. As applies to other south-east Asian countries, the chances of dealing with ethnic Chinese in private business circles are high. As most Indonesian Chinese are non-Muslim, two principal cultures will be encountered.

Country background

Population

The population of Indonesia is 220 million, 70% of whom live on Java, the fifth largest island in the archipelago.

Ethnicity and religion

Indonesia has the largest Islamic population in the world, with over 90% being Muslim. Javanese is the largest ethnic group, accounting for around 40% of the total population. Ethnic Chinese comprise 4% of the population and 70% of these follow the Christian faith. There are also over 250 different ethnic groups spread around the many islands of the archipelago.

Language and script

Over 30 different languages and many more dialects are spoken throughout Indonesia. Owing to the fact that over the years there was suppression of Chinese culture in Indonesia, many local Chinese do not speak Mandarin or any other Chinese dialect.

The *lingua franca* of the country is *Bahasa Indonesia*, the basics of which were introduced from Malaysia. Although the primary languages of both Indonesia and Malaysia are similar, *Bahasa Indonesia* has some Dutch nuances, following early Dutch occupation of the country. The written form of *Bahasa Indonesia* uses the same alphanumeric characters as English, and being non-tonal is relatively easy to learn.

Indonesian words are also easy to pronounce, as most letters have the same phonetic sounds as the English alphabet. Prior to 1972, certain letters and combinations of letters were used to produce specific phonetic sounds, but these were subsequently changed:

Pronunciation	Before 1972	After 1972
"Y"	J	Y
"J"	DJ	J
"OO"	OE	U
"CH"	TJ	C

Thus words with slightly different spellings will be pronounced the same. For instance, it is possible to see the former President Suharto's name also spelled "Soeharto". The family name Widjaja is pronounced "Wijaya". The letter "C" followed by a vowel assumes the sound "CH", e.g. the geographic areas of Cikini and Cilegon are pronounced "Chikini" and "Chilegon".

English is generally spoken, and widely used in international business. Older members of the community may also speak Dutch.

Regional structures

Indonesia is divided into 27 provinces, including three special provinces of Aceh, Jakarta and Yogyakarta. A governor heads each province.

Political environment

Until 2004, there were two legislative houses in Indonesia. The House of Peoples' Representatives comprised 400 democratically-elected seats, plus 100 military appointees. This house enacted government legislation. The Peoples' Consultative Assembly included all members of the House of Peoples' Representatives, plus another 500 appointees from various parties and regions. The House of Representatives elected the president, who then appointed cabinet ministers.

The significant military presence in the government originates from the days of an earlier president, Suharto, who being an army general bulldozed his way into the leadership during the 1960s. To entrench his power he introduced the military into the House of Peoples' Representatives. There is no doubt that over time, this made it difficult for subsequent presidents to control the country as they would have wished, as the military essentially controlled policy decision-making.

In 2004, in order to further democracy and reduce levels of corruption, the ruling president Megawati Soekarnoputri modified the electoral process so that the populace could vote for the president. This is now performed through two rounds of voting. The first is to elect parties in the legislature. The elected parties then select two candidates to participate in a final runoff public election. Elections are held every five years, with any one president serving a maximum of two terms.

In previous years, the Golkar Party of Former President Suharto and his successors was dominant. This was overturned in 2001 when Megawati came to power under her Indonesian Democratic Party of Struggle (PDI–P). Political jostling in the 2004 presidential election runoff saw Golkar officially supporting Megawati, but many members crossed the floor to support the victorious opposition candidate, Susilo Bambang Yudhoyono ("SBY").

Religious, cultural and historical influences

Indonesia is the most populous Muslim nation in the world, and the Islamic faith dominates the archipelago. Buddhism and Confucianism, as practised by local ethnic Chinese, are also present. There are pockets of other minority religions concentrated on certain islands. For instance, the region of Nusa Dua, where the island of Bali is found, is mainly Hindu.

Despite the dominance of Islam, Indonesia is not classified as an Islamic state. This is because Islamic ways do not dominate the political system, as they do in Malaysia. Indonesians are free to select their own religion and it is not uncommon to find Christian followers, believed to comprise up to 10% of the population.

Ethnic boundaries

As with other countries in south-east Asia, a large amount of private enterprise in Indonesia is owned by ethnic Chinese. When dealing with government bodies, there is a good chance that Muslims will be encountered. While Chinese prosperity is tolerated in most other countries, there is no doubt that Chinese business people have in the past been singled out for persecution. Fortunately the situation is now changing for the better.

As the outlook and behaviour of Muslims and Chinese are quite different, it is important at an early stage to identify an Indonesian's ethnicity. This is not an easy task, as the groups cannot be distinguished by their names – this is because under the rule of Suharto, many Chinese assumed local names in order to conceal their identity. In some cases Chinese people can be distinguished from Muslims by their lighter complexions.

Islam

Indian traders introduced Islam into Indonesia. The western tip of Sumatra (Aceh) adopted Islam during the 13th century, and thereafter it flowed through to Java during the 16th and 17th centuries. Although today it is practised in a less orthodox form, it is now the professed religion of most Indonesians. Muslims in Indonesia are granted some freedom regarding their lifestyle – for instance, women need not wear a head scarf (*jilbab*) or a long flowing dress (*baju muslim*).

Buddhism

Although Islam is by far the dominant religion of Indonesia, the small Chinese community scattered throughout the archipelago practises Buddhist beliefs of the *Mahayana* sect. This was introduced by Chinese immigrants. In the past, Buddhism was not well tolerated by local Muslims but the situation is gradually improving.

Christianity

In recent years, Christianity among the Chinese group has seen tremendous growth, mainly in the "charismatic" and "free-thinker" forms. This upsurge in Christianity owes its beginnings to the days of Suharto, when in the 1970s he disallowed Confucianism. As citizens were expected to have a formal religion, many Chinese opted for a Catholic or Protestant following. With the recent growth in Chinese wealth, many newer evangelical Protestant churches have capitalised on this opportunity. They promote a trendy lifestyle, and in contrast to Catholicism and Buddhism endorse wealth accumulation by its congregation. Despite their newfound Christian ways, though, ethnic Chinese in Indonesia still have a deep-rooted Asian outlook.

Historical influences

There is evidence to show that man ("Java man") inhabited parts of Indonesia as long as half a million years ago. Immigrants began arriving from 3000 BC onwards, coming from southern China and the Pacific islands. Indian traders first arrived during the 5th century and introduced Hinduism, which eventually found its way to east Java and Bali.

The first significant European presence appeared during the 17th century, when Indonesia was colonised by the Dutch under the Dutch East India Company. Remnants of Dutch culture still exist in the country today. Indonesia remained a Dutch colony until the Second World War when it was invaded by Japan, which ruled it under a harsh and exploitative rule.

Following the end of the War, an attempt by the Dutch to re-colonise Indonesia was thwarted and shortly afterwards the first president, Achmad Sukarno was installed. He ruled with strong support from the military, which to this day has a significant say in political affairs. Sukarno introduced a policy of disengagement from the West, which ultimately resulted in economic chaos.

In 1966 General Raden Suharto displaced Sukarno and was officially elected president. He re-established links with the West and encouraged foreign investment. Under his rule, political stability ensued, but only because of suppression of minority groups and his use of military power. He initiated discrimination against ethnic Chinese under a *pribumi* system, whereby Muslims were given preferential treatment in educational and employment opportunities. This *pribumi* system still prevails today. Suharto ruled until 1998 when he was forced to step down following demonstrations against his nepotism and brutal ways. Despite promises made by Suharto's successors to address rampant corruption in Indonesia, this still remains an endemic problem throughout the country.

Social and business values

Islam plays a major role in the daily lives of most of the population. The need to observe prayer rituals takes precedence over other issues. Links to village-based families in the rural areas are strong, with family demands taking priority over business matters. Slow progress in business from delays caused by personal domestic issues should therefore be expected and tolerated.

As most business in Indonesia is practised on Java, the chances of encountering ethnic Javanese are high. As their origins are mainly agrarian, they do not possess a strong trading background. The Javanese way is to maintain an inner peace and harmony that is not harmed by outside influences.

Bapakism – or recognition of the head (*bapak* or "father") of the family, clan or company is important in Indonesia, creating a hierarchy in both society and business. Junior staff members lack independence in making decisions, deferring to *bapak*. Such bureaucracy can result in significant delays in decision-making.

Loss of face (*malu*) is important in the way Indonesians behave in life. The need to save face among Javanese is an even stronger driving force than it is among other Asian cultures, such as the Chinese. For instance, if someone makes a mistake, particularly in public, an Indonesian may allow them to continue without correcting them, rather than cause them *malu*.

Javanese have a distinct aversion to saying "no"; probably more so than any other Asian culture. However, other ethnic groups such as Sumatrans and Manadonese may be more direct in their manner.

Orders and instructions should not be given in a coarse or aggressive way, with a need to be discreet at all times. Bad news should also not be imparted readily, especially to a senior person – the Indonesian expression for this is *asal bapak senang* or "keeping father happy". Concealment of negative views may be perceived by westerners as lying, when in actual fact the so-called "liar" is only trying to maintain contentment, harmony and peace.

The small ethnic Chinese population has its own set of beliefs, similar to those practised in Greater China and elsewhere in south-east Asia. In order to survive in the *pribumi* climate, local Chinese have had to carve a niche for themselves in both business and society based on hard work and efficiency. By comparison with the Muslim population, they react more quickly and responsively, a trait that has enabled them to successfully compete and survive as a minority. Thus, as with other countries in south-east Asia, a large amount of private enterprise in Indonesia is owned by ethnic Chinese (*sukong*). Their ability to circumvent Indonesian bureaucracy makes them useful business partners.

Many of the generic rules of dealing with Asians apply to Muslims. There is some lack of acceptance of western foreigners (known as *bule*, pronounced "boolay") owing to past dominance of their country by the Dutch. Europeans and Americans should therefore display sensitivity and respect by avoiding loud and arrogant behaviour in the presence of Indonesians. As with other developing countries in south-east Asia, local Indonesians believe that Caucasian westerners are very wealthy and therefore charge over-inflated prices in shops and stores. There is usually a two-tier system of pricing – the "local price" and a much higher "foreign price". To some extent, this line of thinking also prevails in business.

Most business contact in Indonesia will be with males, but this does not mean that women are not considered equal. There is no doubt that women in Indonesia are beginning to play a greater role in business and government circles, e.g. a recent president, Megawati Sukarnoputri, was a woman.

Unfortunately, Indonesia is one of the most corrupt countries in Asia, and business tends to move forward only after "gifts" or "personal discounts" have been made to influential people, usually at their request. This emanated from the days of Suharto, and although still endemic throughout the country, corruption is slowly being eliminated. In government circles, civil servants receive very low wages and receipt of supplementary income from other "non-formal" sources is often condoned. Foreign companies with operations in Indonesia sometimes employ local staff with family connections in key government areas in order to "overcome" administrative hurdles.

The Javanese traits described above make Indonesia an interesting and challenging country in which to conduct business. The need to have influential relationships with the right people in important positions is of overriding importance, but not always easy to establish. Time will be required to identify key people, ascertain their value as potential "movers and shakers", and then cultivate the necessary relationships with them.

Local customs and etiquette

Special beliefs

Western visitors to Indonesia should be aware of the following special beliefs held by the Muslim population:

- The left hand is considered "unclean" and should not be used for giving or receiving. It should also not be used for pointing at a person.
- Green and yellow are favoured colours.
- Consumption of pork and alcohol is forbidden.
- Midday on Friday is the most important time of the week for praying.
- *Ramadan*, the month of fasting, followed by the celebration of *Idul Fitri*, is the most important occasions of the year.
- Great respect should be shown towards the most senior person in families and organisations.
- Muslims are required to wash themselves before their next prayer session. Should they have touched a dog, a more rigorous washing process is required. The hands, elbows, face, head, ears and feet are cleansed.

Etiquette

When interacting with Indonesian Muslims, **don't**:

- Pass an item, especially food, using the left hand – Muslims consider this hand a "dirty hand".
- Shake hands using the left hand.
- Point at or move items on the ground, with the foot.
- Make jocular remarks or criticise the Islamic religion, Mohammed or Allah. The Islamic term *Insh'Allah* ("if God is willing") should also not be taken lightly or denigrated.
- Use the American action of pounding the fist into an open palm of the other hand. This is considered an obscene gesture.

- Point with the forefinger. Rather use the open palm of the hand. Only the right hand should be used for pointing.
- Adopt the pose of hands on hips. This is seen as an extremely aggressive pose (*wayang*).
- Show anger to a superior or disagree with him or her in public – deference should be shown to elders and seniors at all times.
- Touch a Muslim man if you are female. He will be required to ritually cleanse himself before praying again.
- Display affection with a member of the opposite gender, in public.
- Cross the legs when seated, or point the soles of the feet towards another person.
- Criticise or praise an Indonesian person in the presence of others – rather do this in private.
- Use colloquialisms or jokes, as these will probably not be understood. If directed at an Indonesian, this may result in an unfavourable face-losing reaction. For example, to refer to someone as a "political heavyweight" might be interpreted as them being obese.
- Be intolerant of a Muslim's need to be excused (even during a meeting) to pray. Be aware that Friday afternoons are a special prayer time.

Preparation and awareness

Appointment scheduling

When preparing to visit Indonesia, the approach for requesting meetings with Chinese and Muslims differs. Muslims prefer to progress business through face-to-face discussions, rather than via written communication. This means that letters of request for appointments, especially during the first phases of contact, may not always be answered. A more personal approach is better, via a facilitator, such as a representative from the embassy or trade commission of your home country, or through a local agent. On the other hand, ethnic-Chinese will be more responsive to written requests and no intermediary is necessary.

Establishing appointments with a senior Indonesian businessman can sometimes be challenging. A secretary will act as his gatekeeper, protecting him from unnecessary and minor disturbances. In most cases, these secretaries are well qualified and experienced women with university degrees. Westerners should endeavour to maintain a healthy relationship with these people, as they wield considerably more power than their counterparts in the West. Tolerance and patience should be exercised, as reports of aggressive behaviour will reach their bosses. This will not lay the foundation for a positive relationship and may cause difficulties in being granted appointments.

In Indonesia appointments should not be scheduled during the following periods:

- The month of *Ramadan* (lunar-based)
  As Muslims fast during this period, productivity tends to slacken. Requests for appointments may be declined.

- *Idul Fitri*, an important holiday period for celebrating the end of *Ramadan*. Many people take the entire week off or return home to rural areas to visit their families.
- *Hari Raya Haji* (occurs shortly after *Idul Fitri*)
  As Muslims travel to Mecca for the *Haj* (the pilgrimage) or simply relax at home, it may be difficult to obtain an appointment at this time.
- Chinese New Year (January/February – lunar-based)
  The Chinese New Year period is not a preferred time to visit Indonesia as most Chinese-owned businesses close over this period.

Although the Islamic weekend normally falls on a Thursday and Friday, in Indonesia, Saturday and Sunday are weekend rest days. However, it should be noted that midday on Friday is an important prayer period for Muslims, and that from this time onwards they may not be available for the remainder of the day.

Unfortunately, as history will show, there have been periods of sporadic unrest and bombings in the centre of Jakarta. Travellers to this city might, depending on the extent of the unrest, wish to postpone their visit. In most cases though, provided due caution is taken and routes through "hot spots" (usually around the university areas and CBD of Jakarta) avoided, safety should not be compromised.

Severe traffic jams in Jakarta and other Indonesian cities often cause lengthy delays. Although distances between addresses may seem short, road networks are intricate systems of one-way streets that require circuitous routes to reach destinations. Allow for plenty of travelling time to reach an appointment.

In order to relieve congestion during morning and evening rush-hours, private cars (not taxis) are required to carry three people ("3 in 1"), which can complicate one's travel arrangements. Locals overcome this problem by hiring street kids from the side of the road, as "riders", to make up the necessary numbers in the car.

Indonesians believe in flexibility when arriving for appointments, known as *jam karet* or "rubber time". In the Indonesian business world, senior managers will keep their juniors waiting. As this process can delay meetings and cause them to overrun, more time should be planned for appointments.

Gifts

When selecting gifts, attention should be paid to the differing gift etiquette of Muslims and Chinese.

Gift-giving in the Muslim world is not as important as it is among other Asian cultures. Owing to attempts by government and private enterprise to stamp out corruption, some Indonesians are circumspect about receiving any gift, even small promotional items, for fear that it may be a bribe.

The following guidelines apply when choosing gifts for Muslims:

- On no account should a gift of alcohol be given. This includes any product containing alcohol, such as a perfume or cologne.
- Items of food should be *halal*, being prepared in a manner that conforms to Islamic tenets.
- Gifts containing pork or products of pigs (i.e. pigskin) should not be given.

- Figurines of dogs, pictures of dogs, toy dogs or anything depicting a dog should not be given. Both pigs and dogs are considered unclean.
- It is not advisable for a man to present a gift to a Muslim woman. If this has to be done, then the man should say that it is a gift from his wife.
- Gifts should be kept as impersonal as possible.
- Green and yellow are preferable (but not essential) colours for gift-wrappings. Avoid white wrapping, as this has funereal connotations.

When selecting gifts for Chinese people, the following items should be strictly avoided:

- Clocks (a sign that death is near).
- Knives, scissors and letter-openers (represents a cut in the relationship).
- Socks, sandals, handkerchiefs and towels (associated with funerals and grieving).
- Flowers, unless they are for the sick, for weddings or for funerals. An even number of flowers should be given.
- Food items should not be presented to the host at the end of a meal, as this implies that the meal was insufficient.
- Any item or congratulatory card depicting a stork, given to the parents of a newborn baby. The Chinese perceive this as a bad omen.

An acceptable gift for an important Chinese person is a bottle of expensive brandy, as this is a common drink that the Chinese enjoy at home. Red wine is also appropriate, as for the Chinese red is symbolic of prosperity and red wine is ostensibly good for the heart.

Gifts should be wrapped in brightly coloured red or yellow paper (preferred). If red paper is used, the red colour should not be too dominant. Purple and white should not be used, as in Taoism these are associated with funerals. An unwrapped gift should not be presented, as this is considered impolite.

Gifts are generally exchanged at the end of a meeting. Discretion is necessary, as there may be situations where presenting a gift to a Muslim might place the receiver in a compromising situation. If senior executives of the Indonesian delegation are present, then gifts may be presented. If middle managers or junior employees are the only persons involved, it may be prudent not to present anything, as this may be perceived as a form of bribery. When presenting a gift to a Muslim or Hindu, it should be given with the right hand. Both hands should be used when presenting gifts to ethnic Chinese.

Dress code

Business attire for men is usually a pair of dark trousers with a light coloured long-sleeved shirt and tie. As Indonesia is close to the equator and the weather is hot and humid all year round, a jacket is not necessary except for more formal occasions. A jacket is acceptable for cool conditions in air-conditioned restaurants.

Women should wear a long-sleeved blouse and knee-length skirt or trousers. Skimpy tops and short skirts are not acceptable. Medium to dark colours should be selected.

Name cards

As English is fairly well understood in Indonesia, and given that *Bahasa Indonesia* uses the same Roman alphabet, it is not necessary to have name cards printed in the local language. However, as academic titles carry recognition in Indonesian business circles, any university qualifications should be displayed. Indonesians sometimes confuse western given and family names. For this reason, family names are sometimes underlined.

Meeting formalities

Names and forms of address

Owing to the large number of ethnic groups in Indonesia, there are many different name structures. Names may comprise one, two or more words. The average citizen may only have one word to their name, while higher-class people will have two or three. To complicate matters further, the family name may appear either first, last or not at all! Some Indonesians do not have family names, based on how the registrar of births entered their name in the records. It is difficult to identify an Indonesian's ethnicity from the appearance of their name, as in the days of President Suharto all Chinese were forced to abandon their ethnic names and adopt Indonesian names. When in doubt, it is advisable to ask an Indonesian by which name they prefer to be addressed.

The Indonesian language has titles of respect that are used in formal situations, including business circles. The titles *Bapak* (shortened to *Pak*) for men, and *Ibu* for women are used, followed by the person's given name. These words literally translate to "father" and "mother".

A male who has completed the *Haj* (pilgrimage to Mecca) may also be known as *Haji*, and a woman as *Hajjah*.

Academic titles are important to Indonesians, and are usually displayed on their name cards. As Indonesia was once a Dutch colony, Dutch academic titles are used. For instance:

- Drs = *Doktorandus*: A male graduate in any field except engineering.
- Dra = *Doktoranda*: A female graduate in any field except engineering.
- Irs = *Insinjur*: An engineering graduate, male or female
- SH = *Sarjana Hukum*: A male or female graduate, with a law degree.

If the person has an academic title, this should be used together with the family name. Below are examples of the most common appearance of Indonesian names (family name underlined) and forms of address:

- Andry <u>Kamajaya</u> ("Pak Andry"): The family name of this man, whose Chinese name should have been Kam Seng Hong, was "Indonesialised" to Kamajaya. "*Jaya*" means successful.
- Djony ("Pak Djony"): Only a single name exists for this Chinese man.
- Bangun Falinda ("Ibu Linda"): This Muslim lady has no family name, and uses the abbreviated form of her second name.

- Bambang <u>Supriatmoko</u> ("Pak Bambang"): In this case, Supriatmoko happens to be the family name.

Fortunately, as a relationship develops, it quickly becomes acceptable to call a person simply by their given name, as is done in the West.

An Indonesian woman usually keeps her name after marriage. However, her children may be given different family names altogether! For example, Former President Suharto's son Tommy, was given the name Hutomo Mandala Putra.

Meeting and greeting

The traditional Javanese greeting is to cross the hands against the front of the chest. They are then raised towards the other person, and then quickly pulled back before contact is made. Fortunately, westerners are not expected to practise this exchange.

In business, handshakes are used when meeting Muslims, but these tend to be limp and held for a longer period than is done in the West. If the person is known to be Chinese a shorter firmer handshake, together with a slight bow, is appropriate. On no account should a western woman initiate a handshake with a man, unless it is evident that the person is Chinese or non-Muslim. To be safe, it is advisable to wait for an Indonesian male to offer his hand first. It is permissible for men to shake hands with Chinese women.

When presenting a name card to a Muslim, it should be passed across with the right hand and on no account should it be presented with the left hand only. It is acceptable to receive the other person's card with both hands, or with the right hand only. This process can make card-exchanging formalities somewhat challenging, as both parties juggle to exchange cards in order to avoid using the left hand! Name cards can be presented to ethnic Chinese using the two-handed technique.

Preliminaries

When arriving for meetings, the Javanese way dictates that less senior delegates should arrive first. Once they have all arrived, the most senior person will make an entrance, commanding much attention from the others as a sign of respect. This means that meetings may start up to thirty minutes late. By observing the delegate arrival order, it may be possible to establish who is the most important decision-maker. To confuse matters further, Indonesians concept of "rubber time" grants them freedom to arrive later than scheduled and to depart for no particular reason during the course of the meeting, only to suddenly reappear again later.

The normal Asian process of selecting seats at the back of a meeting room, so that guests face the entrance, applies in Indonesia. It is recommended that visitors should not seat themselves until invited to do so.

If refreshments are provided, guests should not partake of these until invited to do so by the host. The rule of using only the right hand to eat and drink applies.

Negotiation etiquette

In business today, as most Indonesians are able to speak English, no interpreter should be necessary, but it is advisable to speak slowly and softly. Pausing before replying to another person shows respect – it is extremely rude to interrupt.

Before or after business discussions begin, direct questions about family and personal life may be asked. This is merely a way of building relationships – it would do no harm to reciprocate by asking a few similar questions of the Indonesian party. During this time it may be prudent to enquire from which part of Indonesia they originate. This will provide a useful clue as to their specific ways and how to approach them in future. It is known for instance that the Javanese (from Java) are indirect and reserved, while Manadonese (from Sulawesi) and Sumatrans (from Sumatera) are more direct and approachable.

Information, such as corporate introductions or proposals, should be presented in a humble and discreet manner. Loud and boastful presentations, coupled with a superior attitude, will not be well received. Indonesians are proud people and under such circumstances could feel belittled. In negotiation situations, the other party's status should be elevated, permitting them to feel superior even if they are in a weak position. During stressful times, tempers should be controlled and on no account should voices be raised.

Care should be taken to avoid direct contradictions, in order not to cause loss of face. It is impolite to publicly disagree with someone in a direct way. Westerners should therefore try to be tactfully indirect when correcting an Indonesian. For example, a phrase like "Yes, your idea looks OK, but this could also work ..." is a more discreet way of saying "That is wrong, it should be done in this way".

Knowledge of *Bahasa Indonesia* provides an appreciation of how different phrases are used to avoid difficult situations. Indonesians are able to say "No" in many indirect ways. In *Bahasa*, there are 12 discreet ways of saying "No" which might be interpreted as "Yes" by non-Indonesians. For instance, a remark such as "Yes, this can be done, but it will be difficult" is extremely negative. In some situations, negative news may be imparted subsequent to a meeting, so as to avoid confrontation or loss of face in front of others.

Quick decisions are unlikely to be made during the course of meetings. Indonesians prefer to spend time reaching consensus. Resulting delays can be the cause of much frustration to westerners, who are often under pressure to meet a deadline. Unwritten cultural rules may apply to agreements, even if a written contract is in force. Javanese see a written contract as just one part of the overall relationship, and may not follow agreed contractual terms to the letter. Western businessmen should be prepared to be flexible when negotiating and executing contracts.

Meals and entertainment

Invitations

When dealing with ethnic Chinese, in the spirit of relationship-building, invitations to lunch or dinner are standard practice. However, in the Muslim environment, after-hours entertainment with westerners is not so common. In Indonesia the local host should always be permitted to be the first to extend an invitation. Westerners should therefore be patient, and wait for an invitation to be forthcoming. It is likely that spouses may be invited to dinner, in which case no business should be discussed during the meal.

When extending a meal invitation to a Muslim, care should be taken to select a restaurant that serves *halal* food. Failing this, they will be severely restricted in the food items they can order from the menu.

Food and drink

Food served in the business environment of Indonesia will be either traditional Indonesian or Chinese, depending on the ethnicity of the host.

Westerners will find most Indonesian dishes palatable, although some dishes are quite spicy. Some of the more common dishes are:

- *Nasi goreng*: The local fried rice, mixed with vegetables and spices, and served with a fried egg. In *Bahasa*, *nasi* means rice and *goreng* is the word for fried.
- *Mie goreng*: The equivalent of *nasi goreng*, but made from noodles (*mie* means noodles).
- *Sup buntut*: Oxtail soup, a local favourite. Crackers, onions and sambals are piled on top of the soup.
- *Gado gado*: A cold vegetarian dish served with a peanut sauce.
- *Satays*: The Indonesian version of kebabs made from beef, lamb or chicken, and served with chunks of cucumber, *nasi puti* (compressed rice) and a peanut sauce.

Other dishes containing chicken (*ayam*), fish (*ikan*), beef (*daging*) and squid (*cumi-cumi*, but pronounced "choomee choomee") are quite popular:

- *Daging rendang*: Cubes of beef in a spicy sauce.
- *Ayam rendang*: Chicken pieces in a spicy sauce
- *Ikan goreng*: A fish stew.

Indonesian dishes will not contain pork.

Although Indonesia is a Muslim country, alcohol is freely available. However, unless a host orders and partakes of alcohol himself, only non-alcoholic drinks should be consumed at the table.

Table etiquette

At Indonesian restaurants, guests are seated on chairs around a square or circular table. Diners usually order their own dishes, and meals are not shared. Meals are normally eaten with a spoon and fork, the fork in the left hand and the spoon in the right. The fork is used to push food onto the spoon, which is then used to transfer the food to the mouth.

Table etiquette dictates that:

- The left hand should not be used to pass dishes or other items around the table.

◻ The American manner of using an upturned fork in the left hand to shovel food into the mouth is not considered polite, in terms of Muslim table etiquette.

◻ The right hand should always be used to transfer food and drink to the mouth.

Many Indonesians smoke, and to facilitate this, smoking in most public places, including restaurants, is permitted. Although it is customary to smoke after a meal, it is considered polite to ask for permission to do so beforehand. Cigarettes in Indonesia (*gudang guaram*) are made from tobacco, cloves and herbal sauce. They are also known as *kretek*, a description of the cracking sound they make when lit. *Kretek* leave a strong residual odour, which often pervades the lobbies of hotels and restaurants. Although westerners may find the fragrance quite strong and acrid, it should be politely tolerated.

Where Chinese food is offered in Indonesia, the usual processes and etiquette applicable to meals in the Chinese environment is followed.

Evening entertainment

Owing to the strict limitations on drinking among Muslims, it is unlikely that after-dinner entertainment will be offered and diners will go their separate ways once the meal is over. However, should the host party be Chinese, visits to *Karaoke* bars or nightclubs may be suggested. As this presents a further opportunity for relationship-building, such invitations should not be refused.

Visiting foreigners may be entertained in several nightlife areas, the most prominent being along Jalan Kemang where many restaurants and handicraft shops are located. A more salubrious area of nightclubs and massage parlours is situated along Mangga Besar and is frequented mainly by locals, although westerners may also be hosted here.

9 Malaysia

Malaysia is geographically spread over two distinct regions, named West Malaysia (or "Peninsula Malaysia") situated south of Thailand on the main Asian continent, and East Malaysia, located on the northern part of the island of Borneo (now called Kalimantan). Malaysia shares Kalimantan with both Indonesia, and the small but wealthy state of Brunei.

The country proclaims itself as "Malaysia, truly Asia". As implied from this catch phrase, the country is an interesting blend of Asian cultures. Although predominantly Muslim, Malaysia has a significant Chinese population. It is governed along Islamic principles and is the second largest Islamic country in Asia, behind Indonesia.

As applies to most other south-east Asian countries, the Chinese tend to play a dominant role in local private business, so the chance of interacting with them is extremely high. Although people of Indian origin are a minority in Malaysia, they may also be encountered in business.

Country background

Population

The population of Malaysia is 22 million, most of whom (85%) live in West Malaysia.

Ethnicity and religion

East and West Malaysia have a population that comprises Malay (Muslims, 58%), Chinese (27%), Indian (8%) and others (7%). Roughly 1% of the population are indigenous tribes (*orang asli*). In early Malaysian history, intermarriage between Malay and Chinese, particularly around the western port of Melaka, created an interesting Peranakan subculture.

Islam is dominant in the Malay community, while Buddhism and Taoism is practised by the Chinese. Although the Indian community is mainly Hindu, some Muslim sects also exist.

Language and script

The Malay people speak *Bahasa Malaysia*, a relatively simple and easy language to learn, as it uses the English alphabet. Pronunciation of certain letters is, however, different:

"UA" is pronounced with a "W" sound,

e.g. *tuan*, meaning gentleman, is pronounced "twun";

"C" followed by a vowel is pronounced "CH",

e.g. *cempaka*, a local flower, is pronounced "chempaka".

An interesting feature of *Bahasa Malaysia* is that plurals repeat the specific noun. For instance, the plural of lady (*puan*), is "puan puan".

Mandarin is spoken among the Chinese, with the main dialects being Hakka, Hainanese, Hokkien and Teochew, all from the southern part of China. The Indian population speaks mainly Tamil and some Hindu.

English is commonly spoken and is widely used in international business, although in rural areas it may not be clearly understood.

Regional structures

The country is divided into 13 states, with 11 situated on West Malaysia and two on East Malaysia. There are two federal districts of Kuala Lumpur and Pulau Labuan. Nine states are ruled by a sultan (*yong di-petuan agong*) while the others (Melaka, Penang, Sabah and Sarawak) are ruled by governors (*yong di-petuan negeri*). The states of Terengganu, Kedah and Kelantan are the most Islamic.

Political environment

Malaysia is a federal parliamentary democracy with a constitutional monarch. It is a member of the British Commonwealth. The nine sultans elect among themselves a king (*agong*), who rules for a five-year term.

The head of government is the prime minister. There are two legislative houses, being the senate, comprising 70 members (40 nominated by the king and 30 elected by the legislature), and a 180-member House of Representatives (People's Council). Elections are held every five years. The ruling party is the strong United Malays National Organisation (UMNO). One of the main goals of UMNO is to perpetuate transfer of possession of more than 30% of the country's wealth to Malays, by way of a *bumiputera* system. This process preferentially advances Malays at the expense of other minorities, such as the Chinese, who still hold a high proportion of the country's wealth.

The People's Council holds the legislative power, all of which has to be ratified by the king. The king also has the power to veto the election of a new prime minister.

Religious, cultural and historical influences

Malaysia is classified as a Muslim state, where religion plays a significant role in politics. Its Islamic beliefs are more orthodox than other south-east Asian countries, such as Indonesia. As the country has a significant Chinese population, as well as a minority Indian group, Buddhism and Hinduism are also present.

Ethnic boundaries

As the ways and customs of Chinese, Malays and Indians are different, it is important to correctly identify the cultural background of a Malaysian.

Chinese people tend to have lighter complexions and are slimmer in build than Malays. Malay women are identifiable by their brightly coloured, loose-fitting long dresses (*baju kurung*) and headscarves (*tudung*). Malay men sometimes wear a black or white brimless hat called a *songkok*. A white *songkok* signifies that the wearer has completed the *Haj*.

It is possible to identify Malays from their names, which are quite distinctive from those of the Chinese and Indians. When dealing with government bodies, there is a good chance that Malays will be encountered. Indians in Malaysia are easy to identify by their ethnic features, with most of them originating from southern India.

Sikhs, followers of a religious hybrid of Hinduism and Islam, may also be encountered in Malaysia. They can be identified by their thickset physiques, beards and coloured turbans.

Islam

Islam was introduced into Malaysia during the 14th century, with the arrival of Arab traders. Since then it has emerged as the dominant religion and spread throughout the country. Some states are far more orthodox than others. For example, the West Malaysian states of Kelantan and Terengganu are more strict with regard to observation of the rules of the *Qur'an*.

Taoism and Confucianism

The Chinese beliefs of Taoism and Confucianism were brought to Malaysia with the arrival of immigrants during the 19th century. In terms of open worship, Taoist beliefs prevail, as can be seen by the number of temples around Malaysia. Although there is not much open worship of Confucianism, its principles are ingrained in the lives of most Malaysian Chinese.

Buddhism and Hinduism

Mahayana Buddhism, imported from India in the 1st century AD, is also practised by the Chinese population. Hinduism, the main religion of the minority Indian population, was introduced at the same time. Both these religions preceded Islam, which only appeared much later.

Historical influences

The earliest of the present-day ethnic people (*orang asli*) were found on peninsular Malaysia over 5 000 years ago. The first Malay settlers, thought to come from southern Indo-China and Austronesia, arrived in 1000 BC.

During the 5th century the Melaka straits on the West Coast of the peninsula were established as entrepôts – storage ports to cater for the needs of passing vessels.

In 1511 Melaka was captured by Portugal and remained under its control for the next 130 years, until in 1641, after a five-month siege, Holland gained control over this strategic port. By 1795, the Dutch had lost control to the British, who proceeded to set up bases in Penang, Melaka and Singapore, naming them "The Straits Settlements", and then later "British Malaya". The British encouraged Chinese and Indian immigrants to work on rubber plantations and in tin mines.

During the Second World War, Japan invaded Malaya. Following the Japanese surrender, Britain resumed its authority in the region and formed the Malay Union. Singapore became a separate crown colony.

In 1946, to restrict progress of Chinese and Indian immigrants, Malay nationalists formed the United Malays National Organisation (UMNO). UMNO's objective was to promote special privileges for Malays in society and business. In 1971, UMNO promulgated a New Economic Policy (NEP) whereby ethnic Malays were classed as *bumiputeras* ("sons of the soil") and given preferential positions in government, commerce and other professions. This practice still prevails, with the objective of transferring 30% of the country's wealth to Malays. Currently the figure stands at 19%.

In 1957 Britain relinquished its control of Malaya and the first prime minister, Tunku Abdul Rahman, was installed. A brief administrative association with Singapore in 1963 lasted only two years before the two split into Malaysia and Singapore as they are today.

Social and business values

Three ethnic groups exist in Malaysia, the largest being Malay, then Chinese and finally Indian.

Most of the generic rules of dealing with Asians apply to Malays. However, their practice of the Islamic faith does influence their behaviour in business. Although in Middle Eastern Islamic states men play a greater role in business than women, in Malaysia women can be found in influential business positions.

In order to survive in the *bumiputera* climate, the local Chinese have had to carve their own niche in business, based on hard work and efficiency. Thus, as with other countries in south-east Asia, much private enterprise in Malaysia is owned by the ethnic Chinese.

While business dealings with Chinese will generally happen in a fast and efficient manner, the pace when dealing with Malays may be somewhat slower and subject to variability. In some ways, the Muslim belief that Allah will dictate what will happen and when (*Insh'Allah*) may influence the outcome and timing of events. Malays observe prayer rituals that often take precedence over other issues, particularly at midday on Friday.

Malays believe that Caucasian westerners are very wealthy, and that they can therefore charge over-inflated prices in shops and stores. There is usually a two-tier system of pricing – the "local price" and a much higher "foreign price". To some extent this line of thinking also prevails in business.

Face-saving influences the way all Malaysians behave in business. The need for Malays to avoid loss of face is an even stronger driving force than it is among the Chinese. This manifests itself in the way Malays behave when faced with conflict situations, or when they do not understand an instruction. They display a great reluctance to saying "no" or openly disagreeing. Instead, a subtle, indirect strong negative response might be given, which can be misleading to an uninformed westerner. There have been many occasions when Malays have acted contrary to an "understanding", leading to confusion and frustration. When instructing Malays, care should be taken to ensure that this is not done in a paternalistic or aggressive way. As it is face-losing in the Malay world to admit that one does not understand, it may be necessary to double-check that instructions have been comprehended.

The Indian population of Malaysia originates from different parts of south Asia, revealing many different cultures, each with their own unique set of values. The two most common religions are Hindu and Islam. When dealing with Indians, it is therefore essential to determine their religion, as aspects of their etiquette differ. Most Indians in the business world are fairly westernised and easy to work with.

Local customs and etiquette

Special beliefs

Western visitors to Malaysia should be aware of the following special beliefs of the Muslim population:

- ◻ The left hand is considered "unclean", and should not be used for giving or receiving. It should also not be used to point at a person.
- ◻ Green and yellow are favoured colours.
- ◻ Consumption of pork and alcohol is forbidden.
- ◻ Midday on Friday is the most important time of the week for praying.
- ◻ *Ramadan* (*Hari Raya Puasa*), the month of fasting, followed by the celebration of *Hari Raya Aidilfitri*, is the most important event of the year.
- ◻ Great respect should be shown towards the most senior person in families and organisations.
- ◻ Muslims are required to wash themselves before their next prayer sesson. Should they have touched a dog, a more rigorous washing process is required. The hands, elbows, face, head, ears and feet are cleansed.
- ◻ Unmarried couples are not permitted to engage in intimate contact before marriage, and should not spend time alone together without a chaperone.

The following important beliefs apply to the Chinese population of Malaysia:

- ◻ The number four is considered very unlucky, as it is associated with death (the Mandarin pronunciation of "four" and "death" are nearly identical).
- ◻ The number eight or any combination of eight (such as 8888), is considered very lucky.
- ◻ "X" or a cross signifies death. A person's name or picture should never be marked with a cross. The act of crossing chopsticks or any act that can result in the appearance of a cross is considered an omen of impending death.
- ◻ The colours red (prosperity) and yellow (gold, wealth) are desirable colours. Green is also acceptable, signifying longevity. Dark purple, dark blue, white and black are not considered favourable.
- ◻ Flowing water implies that money will flow into a business, which is why many Chinese businesses in Malaysia have a water feature at the entrance to their premises.
- ◻ Creatures also have significant meaning:

- A dragon implies great strength and power.
- Tortoises symbolise long life.
- Fish are a sign of prosperity, which is why the Chinese often keep fish in tanks either at home or in the office.
- A pair of lions may often be seen guarding the door of a Chinese enterprise. This is to keep evil spirits at bay.

In the case of the minority Hindu population, the following special beliefs apply:

- As with Muslim beliefs, the left hand is considered unclean.
- Beef products are not widely consumed. Many Hindus are vegetarian.
- Products made from cowhide, such as leather, are not used or bought.
- Books are considered sacred, and should not be desecrated or mishandled.
- Smoking is not permitted, by Sikhs or Indian women.
- Married women wear a red dot in the centre of their foreheads.
- Fridays are important for temple visiting. Fruit offerings of bananas or coconuts are often made.

Etiquette

When interacting with Malays, **don't**:

- Pass an item, especially food, using the left hand – Islam considers this hand a "dirty hand".
- Shake hands using the left hand.
- Point at or move items on the ground, using the foot.
- Touch a person on the head, children included, as this is considered the most sacred part of the body.
- Make jocular remarks or criticise the Islamic religion, Mohammed or Allah. The Islamic term *Insh'Allah* ("if God is willing") should also not be taken lightly or denigrated.
- Use the American action of pounding the fist into the open palm of the other hand. This is considered an obscene gesture.
- Point with the index finger. Rather use the open palm of the right hand, or better still, make a fist keeping the thumb at the top of the fist and point with the thumb. Only the right hand should be used for pointing.
- Wink at a Malay, particularly not at a woman.
- Adopt the pose of arms akimbo on the hips. This is seen as an extremely aggressive pose.
- Show anger to a superior, or disagree with a superior in public – deference should be shown to elders and seniors.
- Praise Singapore in front of Malays – this will harm Malay pride.
- Touch a Muslim man if you are female. He will be required to ritually cleanse himself before praying again.
- Display affection, in public, with a member of the opposite sex.
- Cross the legs when seated, and avoid pointing the soles of the feet towards another person.

◻ Be intolerant of a Muslim's need to be excused (even during a meeting) to pray, and be aware that 11 am to noon on Friday is a special prayer time for men.

The following procedures should also be noted:

◻ When passing in front of someone or between two people, particularly if they are older or more senior, it is considered polite to bend forward slightly.

◻ In the interests of cleanliness and hygiene, shoes should be removed when entering a Malay home. This is because they usually sit on the floor when socialising and praying.

When interacting with Malaysian Chinese, **don't**:

◻ Use the crooked index finger to beckon someone; rather use the standard Asian method of palm down and flapping the hand.

◻ Write a person's name in red ink; this signifies that they will die.

◻ Wink at a person.

◻ Present items such as name cards, gifts, cash notes and credit cards with one hand – this should be done with both hands.

◻ Criticise Singapore to Malaysian Chinese. Some Chinese working in Malaysia are from Singapore. Malaysia–Singapore relations can at times be a sensitive issue.

◻ Display your feelings through facial expression. The Chinese are adept at interpreting a person's inner feelings via body language and facial expression.

When interacting with Malaysian Indians of the Hindu faith, **don't**:

◻ Throw about or abuse books.

◻ Gesture at a person with the forefinger. Rather use the open hand.

◻ Pat a child on the head.

◻ Pass items across with the left hand.

◻ Smoke in the company of a Sikh.

Preparation and awareness

Appointment scheduling

While the Chinese and Indians will be responsive to written requests for appointments, Malays prefer to progress business through face-to-face discussions. This means that letters of request for appointments, especially during the first phases of contact, may not always be answered. A more personal approach would be better and a facilitator, such as a representative from the embassy or trade commission of a home country, or an agent, should be engaged for this purpose.

Appointments should not be scheduled in Malaysia during the following periods:

◻ The month of *Ramadan* (lunar-based)

As Muslims fast during this period, productivity tends to slacken. Requests for appointments may be declined.

◻ *Hari Raya Aidilfitri*, an important holiday period of festivities to celebrate the end of *Ramadan*. Many people take this entire week off to return to the rural areas and to visit their families.

◻ *Hari Raya Haji* (February)

As Muslims travel to Mecca for the *Haj* (pilgrimage) or simply relax at home, it may be difficult to obtain an appointment at this time.

◘ Chinese New Year (January/February – lunar-based)

The Chinese New Year period is not a preferred time to visit Malaysia, as most Chinese-owned businesses and operations close over this period.

The Islamic weekend is normally a Thursday and Friday. In most Malaysian states, Saturday and Sunday are weekend rest days. However, in the three most Islamic states of Kedah, Kelantan and Terengganu, Friday and Saturday are promulgated weekend days, with Sunday being the first day of the working week. Throughout Malaysia, midday on a Friday is an important prayer period, and from this time onwards Malays may not be readily available.

In the capital city of Kuala Lumpur traffic jams can cause delays, especially during rush hours and particularly when it rains. Unfortunately, as most road signs in Malaysia are not displayed in English, road navigation is not easy and the chance of getting lost is high.

Malays believe in flexibility when arriving for appointments and may not always appear on time. Therefore, some contingency time should be allowed when scheduling appointments. If appointments are being arranged around the outskirts of Kuala Lumpur or in smaller towns, it is recommended that a taxi be retained on an hourly basis, as taxis in these areas are not always freely available.

Gifts

When selecting gifts, attention should be paid to the various Malaysian ethnic groups (Muslim, Chinese and Hindu), as their gift etiquette differs.

Gift-giving procedures in the Malay world are not as important as they are among other Asian cultures. Owing to attempts by government and private enterprise to stamp out corruption, some Malays are circumspect about receiving any gift, even small promotional items, for fear that it may be a bribe.

The following guidelines apply when choosing gifts for Malays:

◘ On no account should a gift of alcohol be given. This includes any product containing alcohol, such as perfumes and colognes.

◘ Items of food should be *halal*, being prepared in a manner that conforms to Islamic tenets.

◘ Gifts containing pork or products of pigs (i.e. pigskin) should not be given.

◘ Figurines of dogs, pictures of dogs, toy dogs or anything depicting a dog should not be given. Both pigs and dogs are considered unclean.

◘ It is not advisable for a man to present a gift to a Malay woman.

◘ Gifts should be kept as impersonal as possible.

◘ Green and yellow are preferable (but not essential) colours for gift-wrappings. Avoid white wrapping paper, as this has funereal connotations.

When selecting gifts for Chinese people, the following items should be strictly avoided:

◘ Clocks (a sign that death is near).

◘ Knives, scissors and letter-openers (represents a cut in the relationship).

- Socks, sandals, handkerchiefs and towels (associated with funerals and grieving).
- Flowers, unless they are for the sick, for weddings or for funerals. An even number of flowers should be given.
- Food items should not be presented to the host at the end of a meal, as this implies that the meal was insufficient.
- Any item or congratulatory card depicting a stork, given to the parents of a newborn baby. The Chinese perceive this as a bad omen.
- A green hat or cap when presented to a man – this rather strange belief signifies that the wearer's wife is having an affair with another man.

An acceptable gift for an important Chinese person is a bottle of expensive brandy, as this is a popular drink among the Chinese at home. Red wine is also appropriate as red is symbolic of prosperity.

Gifts should be wrapped in brightly coloured red or yellow paper. If red paper is used, the red colour should not be too dominant. Purple and white should not be used, as in Taoism these are associated with funerals. An unwrapped gift should not be presented, as this is considered impolite.

The following considerations apply when selecting gifts for Indians of the Hindu faith:

- Gifts of leather, such as wallets or key rings, should not be given.
- When money is given as a gift, an odd amount should be presented, as a sign of good luck.
- Avoid giving a gift containing even numbers of the same item.
- Frangipani or white flowers should not be given, except at funerals.
- Liquor, cigarettes or ashtrays should not be given to Sikhs.
- Avoid wrapping gifts in paper that is white or black. Red, yellow and green are preferable.

Gifts are generally exchanged at the end of a meeting. In the case of Malays, this should be done using the right hand, with the left arm supporting the right arm. For Chinese recipients, the gift should be presented using both hands. When giving a gift to an Indian person, it should be presented with the right hand supported by the left hand.

Dress code

Business attire for men is usually a pair of dark trousers with a white or light coloured, long-sleeved shirt and tie. As Malaysia is close to the equator and the weather is hot and humid all year round, a jacket is not necessary except for more formal meetings. Women should wear a conservative long-sleeved blouse and knee-length skirt or trousers, particularly if it is known in advance that the party to be met will comprise Malays. Skimpy tops and short skirts are not acceptable. Medium-to-dark colours should be selected.

Name cards

As English is well understood in Malaysia, and given that *Bahasa Malaysia* uses the same Roman alphabet, it is not necessary to have name cards printed in the local language. Malaysians sometimes confuse western given and family names. For this reason, family names are sometimes underlined.

Meeting formalities

Names and forms of address

Each of the three main ethnic groups of Malaysia has its own distinct name structure, from which their ethnicity can be determined.

Malays have a sophisticated and complex system of names and titles that span the entire social strata. Foreigners will find interpreting a Malay person's name extremely challenging, as there are many different combinations of names and titles.

Bin and binte

Malay names comprise a personal given name, followed by the father's given name. Thus the basic name structure for Malays is:

{Own given name} {father's given name}, e.g. Mansor Rahmat.

Sometimes the word *bin* (male) or *binti/binte* (female) will be inserted between the two names. *Binte* is abbreviated to *bt* or *bte*. These small Arabic words mean respectively "son of" and "daughter of" the father whose given name appears at the end,

e.g. Mansor bin Rahmat; Mansor, son of Rahmat or Haslina bt(e) Ibrahim; Haslina, daughter of Ibrahim.

To complicate matters further, some Malay women assume their husband's name, in which case *bte* will be excluded. In recent times some Malay women have begun adopting both their husband's and their father's names, combined into a hyphenated word.

Mr, Mrs and Miss

When addressing a Malay, the father's given name (usually the last word of the name structure) is never used.

In everyday life, the Malay forms of address for Mr, Mrs and Miss apply to those who do not enjoy elevated status. These are respectively *Encik, Puan* and *Cik*, followed by their given name. In Malay, "C" is pronounced "CH", such that *Encik* is pronounced "enchik" and *Cik* is pronounced as "chik". The "U" in "UA" is pronounced like a "W", so that *Puan* is pronounced "pwunn". It is quite acceptable to address an unmarried female as *Puan,* as this is also considered a sign of respect,

e.g.: Mansor bin Rahmat = "Encik Mansor"; Haslina bt(e) Ibrahim = "Puan Haslina".

In normal business circles in Malaysia, it is possible to dispense with the use of *Encik* and *Puan* fairly early in the relationship and simply use given names, as would be done in the West.

Clan and royal names

In certain cases a prefix to a given name may appear. This may be *Nik*, *Shah*, *Wan Megat* or *Putri*, to name a few. These are either clan or family names, or names that are indirectly associated with Malay royalty,

e.g.: Wan Rusli bin Wan Muhamad is referred to as "Encik Wan Rusli", or "Wan Rusli"; Putri Nooraini Ibrahim is called "Puan Putri Noorani", or "Putri Nooraini".

Religious names

Some Malay people may also carry a religious title. The most common of these are: *Haji* (female: *Hajjah*): a person who has completed the *Haj* to Mecca and *Syed* (female: *Sharifah*): a religious title passed down through the family. This implies that the person is a descendant of the Prophet Mohammed.

In such cases, a person should be granted a more courteous form of address, such as *Tuan* (pronounced "twunn") for a man, and *Puan* for a woman,

e.g.: Haji Hamzah bin Sulong becomes "Tuan Haji Hamzah". This may be shortened to just "Tuan Haji" or, in the case of a woman, to "Puan Hajjah". Similarly, Syed Alwi Abdullah would then be called "Tuan Syed Alwi".

Sometimes the name *Mohammed* (abbreviated form *Mohd*) or *Nur* (female) may be seen at the beginning of a name. This should be ignored, and only the following name used,

e.g.: Mohd Nor Abdullah is referred to as "Encik Nor" or "Nor"; Nur Hanisah Ibrahim is referred to as "Puan Hanisah".

Conferred titles

In Malaysia it is quite common for governors or royal heads of state to honour important dignitaries and senior business people in the country with non-royal titles and rankings. The king may confer the following titles:

Tun means "The Most Fortunate" and is the Malay equivalent of "Sir" or "Lady". The wife of a *Tun* is called *Toh Puan*.

A slightly lower ranking ("The Fortunate") is *Tan Sri* (his wife is called *Puan Sri*). Note that the word "Tan" bears no resemblance to the Chinese family name, commonly found in both Malaysia and Singapore. *Sri* can also be spelt *Seri*.

The next rankings are: *Datuk*, conferred on a man by the governor of one of the four states Sabah, Sarawak, Penang or Melaka; or *Dato'*, being conferred on a man by the *agong* or a royal head of state (sultan). *Datin* is the female equivalent of *Dato'*, conferred on a lady who has earned the title in her own right. In the case of a woman married to a man with a conferred title, the following words will appear at the beginning of her name: *Tok Puan* = the wife of a *Datuk*; *To' Puan* = the wife of a *Dato'*.

Many combinations of religious, clan, royal and conferred titles can occur, e.g. Tan Sri Dato' Nik Ibraham Bin Tan Sri Nik Ahmad Kamil. *Tan Sri Dato'* represents a conferred title on a man. *Nik* is the royal or clan family name. Ibrahim is his given name. *Tan Sri Nik Ahmad Kamil* is his father's name. He should be addressed as "Tan Sri Dato'" in conversation, and in writing by his full name. A female example is the name Puan Datin Seri Sharifah Muznah Abdullah. *Puan Datin Seri* means a lady who is either the wife of a *Dato'*, or has earned the title *Datin* in her own right. Sharifah is a religious title. Muznah is her given name. Abdullah is her father's or husband's name. She should be addressed as "Puan Datin Seri" in conversation, and in writing by her full name.

The titles *Tan Sri, Puan Sri (or Seri), Dato', Datuk* and *Datin* can also be conferred on non-Malays. For instance, there are a number of Chinese who have been granted such titles in recognition of their contributions to Malaysia, e.g. Tan Sri Michael Chen.

Senior government officials and royalty

Senior civil servants such as governors, high commissioners, members of parliament and ministers also carry titles of honour. Most of these titles begin with the honorific word *Yang*, followed by more words such as *Berhormat* or *Berbahagia* signifying their status, and are likened to "Your Excellency". They appear as the abbreviations YB and YBhg. Members of the royal family also have the title *Tengku, Tunku* or *Tuanku* at the beginning of their names. The use of these titles is complex and varied, and thus beyond the scope of this book. If any interaction with high-ranking people of extreme honour is anticipated, additional research regarding the application of honorific titles should be undertaken. Where possible, the names of any high-ranking dignitaries to be met should be obtained in advance, together with the correct form of address.

Chinese names

Unlike the Chinese in Indonesia, Malaysian Chinese have been able to retain their original Chinese names. However, they do not always use the *Hanyu pin yin* system devised in China (see Chapter 4, section on "Names and forms of address") in translating their names into the Roman alphabet. Instead they use a direct English translation based on their spoken dialect, which may resemble the *Hanyu pin yin* pronunciation. For instance, the *Hanyu pin yin* name Lin Li Zhu is written in Hokkien as Lim Lay Choo. Chinese names in Malaysia follow the Chinese custom, where the family name appears first, followed by two given names.

The most common Chinese family names are easy to pronounce, such as Tan, Tay, Teo, Yeo, Sim, Lee, Lim and Ong. Another common family name is Ng, pronounced with a nasal "ung" and using a short "u". The name Ooi is pronounced "wee".

For first meetings, a formal form of address using the family name (e.g. "Mr Tan") should be used, but fairly soon afterwards the two first names can be adopted, e.g.: Lim Gim Hai is addressed as "Mr Lim" on a first meeting , but is called "Gim Hai" on a less formal basis.

Sometimes a Chinese man will use the initials of his given names as a means by which he should be addressed, e.g.: Tay Kam Chua may introduce himself as "KC". Women do not follow this practice.

However, many Malaysian Chinese adopt a western given name in addition to their Chinese name. In this case, the western given name appears first, followed by the family name, as applies in western circles. Women sometimes assume hybrids of western female names, such as Vanessia, Jaslyn, Karis, and Olinda, e.g.: Karis Tan is formally addressed "Ms Tan", but once the acquaintance has been made, she may be called "Karis".

A western given name can be displayed together with a Chinese name, either at the beginning or end of the structure, in which case there will be four words. The western name is usually clearly distinguishable, e.g.: Ong Tang Chye David (or David Ong Tang Chye) is informally called "David" in the western context and "Tang Chye" in Chinese.

Women do not take on their husband's name on marriage. Children are, however, given their father's family name. Women can either be addressed "Mrs" or "Ms" if they are married and "Ms" if they are unmarried. Sometimes an older woman may be addressed as "Madam", as a sign of respect.

Although they adopt western given names, many Malaysians are not familiar with how western family names are used. Often they will mistakenly address westerners by their given names, e.g. John Smith might be called "Mr John". In order to avoid confusion between given names and family names, the family name should be underlined on business cards and other correspondence.

Indian names

Traditionally, like Malays, Hindu Indians do not use a family name. Indians of Islamic faith will have a Muslim name, similar to that of Malays.

A male Hindu will use the initial of his father's given name first, followed by his personal name. He will be known as Mr {personal name}, e.g. A Ramalingam will be called "Mr Ramalingam".

Long given names may be shortened for ease of pronunciation. The man in the above example may be called "Mr Ram", or simply "Ram", in less formal circumstances.

Indian females use the same system – her father's initial plus her own personal name. When she marries, the father's initial is dropped and the husband's personal name is added to her own name, e.g. Ms S Thiru marries Mr Patel, becoming Mrs Thiru Patel.

Some Indians originating from Melaka may also have Portuguese names, dating back to the early colonial days, e.g. Alvaro Da Silva will be called "Mr Da Silva".

Sikhs (Indians wearing turbans around their heads) have a given name, followed by the word *Singh* (male) and *Kaur* (female). These are not family names, but are Sikh identifiers. As with the Hindu faith, family names are not used among the Sikh community, thus on no account should Indian Sikhs be addressed as "Mr Singh" or "Ms Kaur".

To trace parentage, the descriptors *s/o* (son of) and *d/o* (daughter of) are used, together with the parents' given name, e.g.: The man Rajen Singh *s/o* Bhopinder Singh is Rajen, son of Bhopinder. Rajen Singh will be called "Mr Rajen Singh" in business circles, and "Rajen" in less formal circumstances. The married woman Baldeva *d/o* Kaur is called "Ms Baldeva Kaur". If Baldeva Kaur married Rajen Singh, she would be addressed formally as "Mrs Rajen Singh", and informally as "Baldeva".

Meeting and greeting

The traditional greeting between Malays is a two-handed handshake, with the hands being released quickly and brought up to the chest. Alternatively, a person will acknowledge another by bringing their right hand across their chest and placing their hand over their heart, as is done when the national anthem is sung in the United States. It is customary to return the gesture.

However, with westerners, the normal handshake is used by Malays, Chinese and Indians. Younger or less senior people take the initiative in greeting elders and superiors, and should not wait for them to initiate a handshake. In the case of Malays, the handshake tends to be limp and held for longer than is done in the West, and only the right hand should be used. On no account should a western woman initiate a handshake with a Malay man – it is advisable to wait for the male to offer his hand, and to allow him to take the initiative. It is even more important that a foreign man should not touch a Malay woman. They are distinguished by the traditional Malay *baju kurung* (a long, brightly coloured loose-fitting dress) and *tudung* (headscarf). If the person is known to be Chinese, then a firmer handshake, together with a slight bow, is appropriate. It is permissible for men to shake hands with Chinese women.

Indian men and women normally use a western handshake when meeting members of the same gender. A man does not normally shake hands with an Indian woman, and a western woman should not offer her hand to an Indian man. In such cases a nod of the head and slight smile can be given.

As age and seniority carry status in Malaysia, the most senior people of a Malay delegation will be introduced first. The western team should follow suit.

Name cards can be presented using the two-handed technique, with the writing displayed the right way up for the recipient to read. A more deferential way is to pass the card across with the right hand, with the left hand supporting the right wrist. On no account should the card be presented using only the left hand. It is also important to receive the person's card with both hands, or just the right hand.

Preliminaries

Meetings with Malaysian Chinese usually start on time. In the case of Malays, meetings may be delayed slightly, as they tend to arrive somewhat later than scheduled.

The Asian process of selecting seats at the back of the meeting room so that guests are facing the entrance, also applies in Malaysia. It is recommended that visitors wait until invited by the hosts, to take their seats.

If refreshments are provided, the Muslim rule of using only the right hand to eat and drink applies. Before or after the discussions, be prepared to field direct questions about family and personal life. This is merely a form of relationship-building – it would cause no harm to reciprocate by asking a few similar questions of the other party.

Negotiation etiquette

As most Malays in business today are able to speak English, no interpreter should be necessary, although it is advisable to speak slowly and softly. Pausing before replying to another person shows respect – it is extremely rude to interrupt. While presenting any information, such as corporate introductions or proposals, it is preferable to be humble and discreet. Loud and boastful presentations, coupled with a superior attitude, will not be well received. Malaysians are proud people and under such circumstances could perceive that they are being belittled. In negotiating situations, the other party's status should be elevated allowing them to feel superior, even if they are in a position of weakness. During stressful times, tempers should be controlled and on no account should voices be raised.

During meetings, in order to prevent loss of face, direct contradictions should be avoided. Even in cases where someone is clearly in error, this should not be pointed out in public. Westerners should therefore try to be tactfully indirect when correcting a Malay. For example, a phrase like "Yes, we can do this your way, but this way might also work…" is a more discreet, face-saving way of saying, "That is wrong, it should be done this way".

Knowledge of the language *Bahasa Malaysia* will facilitate an understanding of how different speech forms can be used for tact. In *Bahasa*, there are many indirect ways of saying "no" which could be interpreted as "yes" by non-Malays. For foreigners with no understanding of the characteristics of *Bahasa*, the real message behind a given answer may not be properly interpreted. A remark such as "Yes, this can be done, but it will be difficult" is extremely negative. Malays avoid conflict during negotiations by initially conceding to a demand, then later following their preferences. Westerners should therefore look out for subtle nuances when concessions are made reluctantly, and anticipate different outcomes.

Quick decisions are unlikely to be made during the course of meetings. Malays prefer to spend time reaching consensus. Such lengthy delays can be the cause of much frustration to westerners, who might be under pressure to meet a deadline.

Meals and entertainment

Invitations

Ethnic Chinese, in the spirit of relationship-building, will usually extend invitations to lunch or dinner. However, in the Malay environment, after-hours entertainment with westerners is not as prevalent. In Malaysia, the local host should always be permitted to be the first to extend an invitation. Westerners should therefore not be pre-emptive in this regard.

When extending a meal invitation to a Muslim, care should be taken to select a restaurant that serves *halal* food. Failing this, guests will be severely restricted in the food items they can order from the menu. It should also be established before meal arrangements are made for Indians whether they are Hindu or Muslim, and if they are vegetarian.

Food and drink

Local meals served in Malaysia will be Chinese, Malay or Indian. Malay and Indonesian cuisine is quite similar. The words *nasi* (meaning rice) and *mie* or *mee* (meaning noodles) appear in many dishes, and provide a clue as to the basis of the meal. *Mie* dishes comprise noodles either "wet" as a soup or "dry", in a fried form. Most dishes tend to be spicy. Some of the most common are:

- *Soto ayam*: A clear chicken soup containing peanuts and chopped spring onion.
- *Nasi goreng*: Fried rice with prawns and vegetables, topped with a fried egg.
- *Nasi lemak*: Rice steamed with coconut milk, served with fried anchovies, peanuts, egg, cucumber and fried chicken or fish.
- *Nasi pandan*: Rice served in a banana leaf.
- *Mie goreng*: Spicy fried noodles made with vegetables, chopped chicken and seafood.
- *Mie reebus*, *mie siam* or *laksa*: Soups of egg noodles, vegetables and egg, in a spicy gravy.
- *Kway teow*: A dish made from fried flat noodles, containing either beef or seafood and mixed with local vegetables.

Other dishes containing chicken (*ayam*), fish (*ikan*), beef (*daging*) and squid (*sotong*) are quite popular:

- *Daging rendang*: Cubes of beef in a spicy sauce.
- *Ayam rendang*: Chicken pieces in a spicy sauce.
- *Ikan goreng*: A fish stew.
- *Sotong sambal*: Squid with curry sambals.
- *Satays*: The equivalent of kebabs made from chicken, lamb or beef, cooked on a charcoal grill. They are served with a peanut sauce, and chunks of raw onion, cucumber and *nasi putih* (steamed rice compressed into cubes).

Malay cuisine will not contain pork products.

Desserts are usually quite simple, consisting of cut fruit like watermelon, papaya and pineapple.

Local Chinese preferences in Malaysia are:

- Hainanese chicken rice: Steamed rice with steamed or roast chicken.
- Chilli/pepper crab: Steamed crab, either whole or in pieces, with chilli or black pepper sauce.
- Dim sum: A light meal, originating from Hong Kong, well recommended at lunch times and comprising small portions of dumplings of pork and prawn.
- "Dry" noodles: Fried noodles, ranging from:
  - *Bee hoon*: Thin vermicelli, fried with shrimp, vegetables and egg.
  - *Char kway teow*: Flat rice noodles, fried with Chinese sausage and a sweet black sauce.
- "Wet" noodles: There are a large variety of soups containing boiled noodles, shrimp, minced fish, beef or vegetables.

One popular sociable meal that Chinese in Malaysia also enjoy is a "steamboat". A gas-heated bowl of boiling water and a hot plate are provided at a table, around which guests sit and cook. Portions of vegetables, seafood and meat, either served at the table or selected from a buffet counter, are cooked in the water or barbequed on the hot plate.

Fortunately, Chinese in Malaysia are averse to eating some of the more challenging and exotic food items consumed in Greater China, but nonetheless there are a few local items that westerners may find difficult to stomach:

◘ Jellyfish: served as a starter, cut into thin strips.
◘ Red baby octopus: served cold and whole, as a starter.
◘ Sea cucumber: white and rubbery, with a strong flavour.
◘ Chicken feet: usually served steamed.
◘ Fish head: served in a curry sauce. The fish eye is considered a delicacy.
◘ Pig's intestines: served boiled in soup.
◘ Shark fin: served in soup.
◘ Abalone: cut into chunks or strips.

From dishes that appear unappetising, only small quantities need be selected. Chinese Malaysians, many of whom spend a lot of time travelling around China, are sensitised to unpalatable forms of Chinese food and are tolerant when westerners decline certain dishes.

While in the western environment, the "white meat", or that away from the bone of chicken and fish is usually preferred, Chinese savour "dark meat" or that attached to the bone. This is why fish head is considered a delicacy.

Dessert is usually cut fresh fruit, although sometimes mango pudding (a kind of mango custard), sago pudding or red bean soup may be served, all of which are quite tasty. At outside eating venues, a fruit called *durian* may be offered. This is a large fruit, similar in appearance and size to a large pineapple. The fruit has a strong pungent and pervading odour, and a flesh that is light yellow with the consistency of raw pastry. While this is a popular local delicacy, many westerners find the combination of its smell and pastry-like consistency quite repulsive.

In the Indian environment, it should be remembered that the cuisine will be based on Muslim, Hindu and also possibly vegetarian requirements. If their belief is Hindu, beef in any form will be forbidden. Cows are considered sacred because they are a source of milk. Muslim Indians will of course not eat pork or any non-*halal* food. Indian food in Malaysia, while spicy, tends to have a more delicate flavour than the usual hot curries that are served in western countries.

Owing to the differing demands of all three principle ethnic groups in Malaysia, many major restaurants offer buffet-style dining which caters for the specific needs of each group.

Although Malaysia is a Muslim country, alcohol is freely available in most of the states. The exceptions are the eastern peninsular states of Kelantan and Terengganu, which are more stringent in observing the Islamic tenets. Alcohol may not be easily obtainable in these regions. Unless Malay hosts offer and partake of alcohol themselves, in deference to their beliefs, only non-alcoholic drinks should be consumed at the table.

Malay table etiquette

For traditional Malay meals, guests are seated on chairs around a square or circular table. When a meal is taken in a Malay home, guests may be seated on the floor. In this instance, a seating style should be adopted whereby the soles of the feet do not point at another person. Men usually sit cross-legged, while women should sit with their legs to the side. Should they be wearing a long dress, the feet should be tucked inside the hem of the dress. Where mixed genders are dining, it is possible that in the Muslim way men and women will be segregated at the table.

In restaurants, meals are normally eaten with a spoon and fork. The fork is held in the left hand, and the spoon in the right. The fork is used to push food onto the spoon, which is then used to transfer the food to the mouth.

The traditional Malay way of eating is with the fingers, but this is not common in normal business circles. At the start of the meal, hands are washed and for this purpose a kettle known as a *kendi* will be provided at the table. The right hand is washed by lifting the *kendi* with the left hand and pouring water over it. Some restaurants also provide a wash basin near the seating area for this purpose. As a backup, it is a good idea to have "wet wipes" available. A drinking glass is placed on the left side of the place setting. In this case it is acceptable to use the left hand for drinking, as the right hand will be soiled by food.

Dishes are normally placed in the centre of the table, and shared. Serving spoons are provided for each dish, and in such cases the left hand is used for serving, should the right hand be soiled. After the main courses, dessert is served. If the dessert is dry without a sauce, hands are used, in which case it will be necessary to wash them again using the *kendi*. If the dessert has a sauce or is sticky, spoons will be provided.

Malay table etiquette dictates that:

- The left hand should not be used to pass dishes or other items around the table.
- Using an upturned fork in the left hand to shovel food into the mouth is not polite.
- The right hand should always transfer food and drink to the mouth. This rule applies even to left-handed people.

Chinese table etiquette

The format and protocols of a Chinese meal in Malaysia are the same as those found in China. Diners are seated around a large circular table, with the most senior host and guest seated at the far side, facing the entrance to the room.

The most senior member of the guest delegation is seated to the right of the most senior host, with the next most senior guest seated on his left. Guests should wait to be allocated seats by their host.

The place-setting usually comprises a bowl for soup, rice or noodles, and a small plate on which to place selected food items. Chopsticks and a flat-based spoon are provided. If difficulty is experienced with chopsticks, it is permissible to pick up the flat spoon with the left hand (for right-handed people), push food onto the spoon using the chopsticks in the right hand, and to then eat from the spoon.

As in China, dishes are shared and not served as individual orders. A large number of dishes are placed in the centre of the table, from which diners may help themselves. Small portions are selected from the main dish, either with chopsticks or a serving spoon, and placed on individual eating plates.

At the beginning of the meal, a number of cold meat or vegetarian appetisers may appear, followed by soup, and then a series of hot dishes, finishing with rice or noodles. Soup is served into each diner's soup bowl, throughout the meal, and then consumed using the flat-bottomed spoon. It is not polite to pick up the soup bowl and drink from it, as is done in Japan. Morsels of food in the soup may be picked out and eaten with the chopsticks or flat-bottomed spoon.

Fish, usually served whole, is divided into pieces at the table. The fish is placed on the table, with its head facing the guest of honour. It is considered bad luck to turn the fish over to access the meat underneath, as in the sailing or fishing environment this portends that a sailing vessel will capsize and sink. The tastiest part of the fish is the head – the eye is considered a real delicacy. The head is reserved for the most important guest, and may be served by the host as a sign of honour. The honoured guest is expected to partake of the flesh (the cheek) from the fish head. When chicken is served, the head of the chicken may also appear on the main serving dish. In this case, it is intended for decoration purposes only and should not be presented to anyone, as it will bring bad luck to them.

Rice or noodles are normally served near the end of the meal, just prior to dessert. These are considered "fillers" in case diners have not had enough to eat during the main meal.

Chinese table etiquette dictates that:

- Guests should allow the host to begin eating first, or wait for the host to invite them to begin eating.
- Pieces selected from the main dish should not be transferred directly to the mouth without first being placed on the eating plate.
- Business should not be discussed during the meal. The time should be used to nurture the relationship, by asking about family life and personal interests.
- Chinese "*ganbei*" toasting is not common in Malaysia. It is acceptable to sip alcohol as would be done in the West, without waiting for a toast.
- It is possible that the host will select some special morsel from the table and place it on a guest's plate. This is a sign of respect, for which thanks should be given. The morsel should be eaten.
- Morsels of food should not be selected from the main serving dish by "picking and hunting" with the chopsticks. The piece to be selected should be visually identified first, before it is taken from the dish.
- Food should not be piled up on the eating plate from the main serving dish.
- It is permissible to stretch across the table from a seated position to select food from a dish. However, it is considered impolite to stand and reach across the table.

- When reaching across to select something from the table, one's arm or chopsticks should not cross that of another person, as this creates an "X" which is a sign of death.
- Once a bite has been taken out of a selected piece of food, it should not be dipped back into a commonly-shared dish of sauce.
- At the end of the meal, a small amount of food should be left on the plate, otherwise the host will continue to offer more food.
- While using a toothpick to remove food particles from the teeth, the mouth should be covered with the hand.

Indian table etiquette

Indian people sometimes eat with their hands, with food being eaten off a single cut banana leaf. A variety of dishes, sauces and condiments are served on the banana leaf, around a centrally placed pile of rice (*nasi daun pisang*). In this format, dishes are not shared. When the meal has been completed, diners will be able to wash their hands at a basin located in an open area in the restaurant.

Indian table etiquette dictates that:

- Only the right hand should be used for transferring food to the mouth.
- It is considered impolite to suck or lick the fingers during the meal.
- Elbows should not be placed on the table.

When the meal is over, the leaf should be folded in half towards the body. The leaf is only folded away from the body at a funeral meal, or if the meal was less than satisfactory.

Evening entertainment

Owing to the strict limitations on drinking among Malays, it is unlikely that after-dinner entertainment will be offered, and diners should go their separate ways once the meal is over. However, should the host party be Chinese, visits to *Karaoke* bars or nightclubs may be suggested. As this presents a further opportunity for relationship-building, such invitations should not be refused.

A popular entertainment area in Kuala Lumpur, the Malaysian capital, is the "Golden Triangle". It is fronted by Jalan Sultan Ismail and is close to Kuala Lumpur city centre, the location of the famous Petronas Twin Towers which, at one time, were the world's tallest buildings.

10 Singapore

Singapore comprises one large island measuring 43 km by 28 km, and over 50 smaller islands, most of which are too small for habitation. It is also the only Asian country that is an island city-state, and by far the smallest country in the region.

It is often said that Singapore is "Asia for beginners" and is certainly a "soft landing" for westerners coming to Asia. It is rated as one of the easiest countries in the world in which to do business, owing to the speed and efficiency of the entire political and economic infrastructure. With no natural resources other than its people, it has recognised the need to create value-added manufacturing and service industries, with an aggressive policy for encouraging western investment and attracting foreign talent. Despite its small size, Singapore has become a major Asian hub for many key industries.

Although first impressions of the country reveal a highly westernised society, there remains a deep underlying Asian culture that is often ignored by foreign executives.

Country background

Population

Singapore has a population of 4.4 million of which 3.3 million are registered as citizens, while the remainder are foreign workers employed as labourers (workmen and domestic servants) or in white-collar jobs. On a daily basis, many Malaysians travel across causeways linking Malaysia and Singapore to work on the island.

Ethnicity and religion

The country is predominantly Chinese (77%), followed by Malay (14%) and Indian (8%). The Chinese population originated from southern China, and are mainly Hokkien and Teochew. The Indian population is mostly south Indian and Tamil.

Over half the population practise Buddhism and Taoism, with 15% being Muslim and 4% Hindu. Approximately 15% of the population, mainly Chinese, is Christian.

Language and script

English is widely spoken in Singapore, and is the official business language. It is taught at "O" and "A" level under the British education system. Being a former British colony and a member of the Commonwealth, there are many remnants of past British influence. For instance many streets, buildings and places in Singapore still have English names.

Most Chinese, except a few older members of the population are fully bilingual, speaking both English and Mandarin. Other Chinese dialects spoken are Hokkien, Teochew, Hainanese and Cantonese, all of which originate from southern China.

Bahasa Malaysia is spoken among the Malays, and Tamil and Hindu is used by most of the Indian population.

Among themselves, local Singaporeans speak *Singlish*, a variation of English based on Chinese and Malay words. *Singlish* uses interesting Chinese grammar structures and metaphors, which gives it a colourful and amusing style.

Regional structures

As Singapore is classified as a city-state, it has no provinces or other regional divisions. Instead, the island has fourteen Group Representative Constituencies (GRC), elected to fairly represent the country's various ethnic and community groups.

Political environment

Singapore is described as a "democratic one-party state". It has a unicameral parliament of nine single members and 75 GRC members, where parliamentary elections are held every five years. It is compulsory to vote. The country, since achieving Independence in 1965, has been under the rule of the People's Action Party (PAP), which was established by Lee Kuan Yew.

The state president is elected by citizens every six years and, in turn, he or she appoints the prime minister, based on a nominations provided by members of parliament.

Religious, cultural and historical influences

By virtue of its large Chinese population, the principle religions of Singapore are *Mahayana* Buddhism and Taoism. A significant number of Chinese also follow various Christian denominations. The Malay group in Singapore are Muslim, while the minority Indians are mainly Muslim or Hindu.

Ethnic boundaries

As the three main ethic groups of Singapore exhibit different traits, it is necessary to identify the ethnicity of a party and apply the appropriate principles of correct behaviour. Chinese people tend to have lighter complexions and are slimmer in build than Malays. Malay women can be identified by their brightly coloured, loose-fitting long dresses *(baju kurung)* and headscarves *(tudung)*. Malay men sometimes wear a black or white brimless hat called a *songkok*. A white *songkok* signifies that the wearer has completed the *Haj*. Malay names are also quite distinctive from those of Chinese and Indian.

Sikhs, Indian followers of a religious hybrid of Hinduism and Islam, may also be encountered in Singapore. They can be identified by their thickset physiques, beards and coloured turbans.

There is a high proportion of Malaysian Chinese living in Singapore, occupying responsible positions in both commerce and government. Because of the *bumiputera* system in Malaysia, which promotes employment and advancement of Malays in favour of other cultures, many Chinese find it easier and more rewarding to work in Singapore.

Malay and Indian people tend to occupy junior positions in the civil service, but some Indians may be found in responsible roles in government, legal and banking circles. Most contact in private enterprise or in government circles is likely to be with Chinese and Indians.

Taoism and Confucianism

The Chinese beliefs of Taoism and Confucianism were brought to Singapore with the arrival of immigrants during the 19th century. In terms of open worship, Taoist beliefs prevail, as can be seen by the number of temples around Singapore. Although there is not much open worship of Confucianism, its principles are ingrained in the lives of most Chinese Singaporeans.

Historical influences

The first mention of Singapore can be found in early Javanese records dating back to the 14th century. These refer to an island settlement at the tip of Malaysia called Temasek ("Water Town"), believed to be a watering point for passing vessels. In 1400 it was renamed Singapura or "Lion City", following a sighting of an animal, possibly a lion, by an Indonesian ruler when he landed there to shelter from a storm.

In 1818, Lord Hastings, the British governor general of India, gave approval for Sir Thomas Stamford Raffles, a successful businessman, to establish a trading post at the southern tip of Malaysia. He arrived in 1819 and concluded a treaty with Temenggong Abdu'r Rahman and Sultan Hussein of Johor, its then rulers, to establish a British trading post on Singapore.

Under Raffles's guidance, Singapore became a major port of call and trading port between Europe and east Asia. By the 1870s, rubber tree plantations on the Malay Peninsula lead to Singapore becoming a major sorting and export centre for natural rubber. Singapore's prosperity led to an influx of immigrants, mainly from southern China. Raffles's influence in putting Singapore on the world map is acknowledged by the many streets, buildings and institutions that still bear his name.

During World War Two Japan invaded Singapore, renaming it Synonto ("Light of the South"). The Japanese commited atrocities against the local population which was forced to adopt Japanese ways. Singapore remained under Japanese control until the end of the War, when British forces returned with a military administration that lasted for only a year. Thereafter, Singapore reverted to being a crown colony of Britain.

Self-government was attained in 1959 following Singapore's first general election. Lee Kuan Yew of the PAP was sworn in as Singapore's first prime minister. Singapore briefly participated in a federation with Malaysia between 1963 and 1965. When the federation was dissolved, Singapore became a sovereign, democratic and independent nation. British protection was finally terminated in 1971. The long British presence in Singapore created a country with many English influences and ways, making it an easy country for foreigners to visit and do business.

Following the federation with Malaysia, Lee Kuan Yew set a vision for Singapore to be a first world country, highly efficient and competitive, through hard work and diligence. Singapore's excellent reputation in the business world of today bears testimony to the successful implementation of his policies.

Social and business values

Over the years, since achieving independence, all Singaporeans have been conditioned to be subservient to the rules and laws of the country, and to be hard working. In what is considered a competitive academic environment, many parents enroll their children for extra classes out of school hours – most free time over weekends and school holidays is spend studying! The discipline and conditioning of such a lifestyle extends to the work scene, where long working hours are the norm.

Singaporeans are mindful of playing by the rules laid down by the local authorities when it comes to consummating business deals. This is contrary to the ways of Chinese elsewhere in south-east Asia, who are adept at circumventing bureaucratic hurdles through sly and subtle means. Thus it is easy to conduct business in Singapore, and processes take place quickly and efficiently.

A large number of Singaporeans study overseas in Australia, the United Kingdom and the United States, and many adopt western customs. However, beneath this western façade, they still have deep-rooted underlying Asian beliefs that should be respected at all times.

Caucasians are termed "Ang Mo", referring to their lighter coloured hair. This is a non-derogatory term that was derived from the early days of British rule.

Chinese Singaporeans have a habit of being *kiasu*, a term used to describe a fear of being left behind. They always strive to be one step ahead of everyone else. This is reflected in their objective to achieve the "Five C's" of materialism – Career, Car (preferably a Mercedes Benz or BMW), Condominium (a luxury apartment as opposed to a government-subsidised flat), Club membership and a Credit card.

Face saving influences the way all Singaporeans behave in business. The need for Malays to avoid loss of face is an even stronger driving force than it is among the Chinese. This manifests itself in the way they behave when faced with conflict situations, or when they do not understand an instruction. They display a great reluctance to saying "no" or openly disagreeing. Instead, a subtle indirect strong negative response may be given, which can be misleading to a westerner. There have been many occasions when Malays have acted contrary to an "understanding", leading to confusion and frustration. When communicating information to Malays, care should be taken to ensure that this is not done in a paternalistic or aggressive way. Because it is considered face losing in the Malay world to admit that one does not understand, it may be necessary to double-check that instructions have been comprehended.

As the Indian population of Singapore originates from several different parts of southern Asia, many different cultures can be found, each with its own unique set of values. The two most common religions are Hindu and Muslim. When dealing with Indians, it is therefore essential to determine their religious following, as some aspects of their etiquette differ.

Local customs and etiquette

Special beliefs

Western visitors to Singapore should be aware of the following important beliefs of the Chinese population:

- The number "four" is considered very unlucky, as it is associated with death (the Mandarin pronunciation of "four" and "death" are nearly identical).
- The number "eight" or any combination of eight (such as 888) is considered very lucky.
- "X" or a cross signifies death. A person's name or picture should never be marked with a cross. The act of crossing chopsticks or any act that can result in the appearance of a cross is considered an omen of impending death.
- The colours red (prosperity) and yellow (gold, wealth) are desirable colours. Green is also acceptable, signifying longevity. Dark purple, dark blue, white and black are not favoured.
- Flowing water implies that money will flow into a business, which is why many Chinese businesses in Singapore have a water feature at the entrance to their premises.
- Creatures also have significant meaning:
  - A dragon implies great strength and power.
  - Tortoises are symbolic of a long life.
  - Fish are a sign of prosperity. The Chinese often keep fish in tanks, either at home or in the office.
  - A pair of lions may be seen "guarding" the door of a Chinese enterprise; this is to keep evil spirits at bay.

The following special beliefs apply to the Malay population of Singapore:

- The left hand is considered "unclean", and should not be used for giving or receiving. It should also not be used for pointing at a person.
- Green and yellow are favoured colours.
- Midday on Friday is the most important time of the week for praying.
- *Ramadan* (*Hari Raya Puasa*) the month of fasting, followed by the celebration of *Hari Raya Aidilfitri,* is the most important event of the year.
- Consumption of pork and alcohol is forbidden.
- Great respect should be shown towards the most senior person in families and organisations.
- Muslims are required to wash themselves before their next prayer session. Should they have touched a dog, a more rigorous washing process is required. The hands, elbows, face, head, ears and feet are cleansed.

In the case of the minority Hindu population, the following special beliefs apply:

- As with Muslim beliefs, the left hand is considered unclean.
- Beef products are not widely consumed. Many Hindus are vegetarian.
- Products made from cowhide, such as leather, are not used.
- Books are considered sacred, and should not be desecrated or mishandled.
- Smoking is not permitted by Sikhs, or Indian women.
- Fridays are important for temple visiting. Fruit offerings of bananas or coconuts are often made.

Etiquette

When interacting with Singaporean Chinese, **don't**:

- Use the crooked index finger to beckon someone; rather use the standard Asian method of palm down and flapping the hand.
- Write a person's name in red ink; this signifies that they are scheduled to die.
- Wink at a person.
- Present items such as name cards, gifts, cash notes and credit cards with one hand – this should be done with both hands.
- Criticise Malaysia to a Singaporean. Many Chinese working in Singapore, although permanent residents of Singapore, are in fact from Malaysia. Malaysia–Singapore relations can at times be a sensitive issue.
- Display feelings through facial expression. Singaporeans are adept at interpreting a person's inner feelings through body language and facial expression.

When interacting with Singaporean Malays, **don't**:

- Pass an item, especially food, using the left hand – Islam considers this a "dirty hand".
- Shake hands using the left hand.
- Point at or move items on the ground, with the foot.
- Touch a person on the head, children included, as this is considered the most sacred part of the body.
- Make jocular remarks or criticise the Islamic religion, Mohammed or Allah. The Islamic term *Insh'Allah* ("if God is willing") should also not be taken lightly or denigrated.
- Use the American action of pounding the fist into an open palm of the other hand. This is considered an obscene gesture.
- Point with the index finger. Rather use the open palm of the right hand, or better still, make a fist keeping the thumb at the top of the fist, and point with the thumb. Only the right hand should be used for pointing.
- Wink at a Malay, particularly a woman.
- Adopt the pose of arms akimbo on the hips. This is considered an extremely aggressive pose.
- Show anger to a superior or disagree with a superior in public – deference should be shown to elders and seniors.
- Touch a Muslim man if you are a female. He will be required to ritually cleanse himself before praying again.

- Display affection to a member of the opposite sex, in public.
- Cross the legs when seated, or point the soles of the feet towards another person.
- Be intolerant of a Muslim's need to be excused (even during a meeting) to pray. Be aware that midday on Friday is a special prayer time for men.

The following procedures should also be noted:

- When passing in front of someone or between two people, particularly if they are more senior than you, it is considered polite to bend forward slightly.
- In the interests of cleanliness and hygiene, shoes should be removed when entering a Malay home. This is because they usually sit on the floor when socialising and praying.

When interacting with Singaporean Indians, **don't**:

- Throw about or abuse books.
- Gesture at a person with the forefinger. Rather use the open hand.
- Pat a child on the head.
- Hand over items with the left hand.
- Smoke in the company of a Sikh.

Preparation and awareness

Appointment scheduling

When first establishing contact with Singaporeans, no third-party introduction is required. Responses to written requests for appointments should be promptly received.

It is convenient to visit Singapore for business purposes at any time of year, except for the Chinese Lunar New Year when there is a two-day holiday. This usually occurs in January or February. Many Chinese take vacations over this period, or go to visit family and friends around the island. However, unlike China which virtually closes down over this period, Singaporeans take shorter breaks with less disruption to the progress of business.

Meetings in Singapore normally commence on time. As there is a fast and efficient road network coupled with a modern underground system, moving around the island is easy, permitting the scheduling of appointments soon after each other, particularly if venues are in the CBD area. Travelling from the centre of the island to the furthest outlying regions requires a maximum travel time of forty-five minutes. The chance of experiencing a traffic jam is low, as the number of cars on the island is carefully regulated.

Gifts

In Singapore, the presentation of gifts is quite common, particularly when interacting with Chinese. The following gifts should, however, be avoided:

- Clocks (a sign that death is near).
- Knives, scissors or letter-openers (represents a severance of the relationship).
- Socks, sandals, handkerchiefs and towels (associated with funerals and grieving).

- Flowers, unless they are for the sick, for weddings or for funerals. An even number of flowers should be given, but not a bunch of four. Flowers should not be given to the mother of a newborn baby.
- A green hat or cap when presented to a man – this signifies that the wearer's wife is having an affair with another man.
- Any item or congratulatory card depicting a stork, given to the parents of a newborn baby. The Chinese perceive this as a bad omen.

Most corporate promotional items are well received. It is not necessary to present an item of great value, and for normal business meetings, token gifts are quite acceptable. For Chinese people, any alcoholic beverage from a home country, especially red wine, will be appreciated.

During the 15 days of the Lunar New Year period, westerners who are well acquainted with a Chinese person who has young unmarried children, can present them with an *hong bao* ("red packet"). One packet is given for each child. *Hong bao* (also written as *ang pau*) are red envelopes with Chinese writing into which money is placed. They can be obtained from most stationery stores. An even number of new, clean currency notes of even denomination should be placed in the packet – an amount in local currency equivalent to US$10 per child is usually sufficient. *Hong bao* can also be given to the parents of a newborn child, to the bride and groom on their wedding day, or by companies to their staff over the Lunar New Year period.

During the months of September and October, it is customary for suppliers and service providers to bring moon cakes when visiting customers. These are round pastries that contain a filling of lotus paste, nuts or the yolk of a hard-boiled egg. They are obtainable at most shops and stalls in Singapore.

The following guidelines apply when choosing gifts for Malays:

- On no account should a gift of alcohol be given. This includes any product containing alcohol, such as perfume or cologne.
- Items of food should be *halal*, and prepared in a manner that conforms to Islamic tenets.
- Gifts containing pork or products of pigs (i.e. pigskin) should not be given.
- Gifts of figurines of dogs, or any picture depicting a dog, should not be given. Both pigs and dogs are considered unclean.
- It is not advisable for a man to present a gift to a Malay woman. If this has to be done, then the man should say that it is a gift from his wife.
- Gifts should be kept as impersonal as possible.
- Green and yellow are preferable (but not essential) gift-wrapping colours. Avoid white wrapping as this has funereal connotations.

Take the following into consideration when selecting gifts for Indians of the Hindu faith:

- No gifts of leather, such as wallets or key rings, should be given to Hindus.
- When money is given as a gift, an odd amount should be presented as a sign of good luck.
- Avoid giving a gift containing even numbers of the same item.
- Frangipani or white flowers should not be used, except at funerals.

- ❑ Liquor, cigarettes or ashtrays should not be given to Sikhs.
- ❑ Avoid white or black gift paper. Red, yellow and green are preferable.

Gifts are normally presented at the end of meetings. These should be suitably wrapped and presented in a gift bag. If the recipient is Chinese, the bag should be presented with both hands. Gifts for Malays and Indians should be given with the right hand, although in Singapore use of both hands is also acceptable. To be absolutely safe, the left hand should never be used to present a gift.

Dress code

Business attire for men is usually a pair of dark trousers with a light coloured, long- sleeved shirt and tie. A short-sleeved shirt, with a tie, is considered casual. As Singapore is virtually on the equator, the weather is hot and humid all year round and jackets are not usually worn, except for very formal evening occasions. A light jacket may be necessary in restaurants with cool air conditioning. Women may wear the normal business attire they would in the West.

Name cards

As English is the main business language in Singapore, it is not necessary to have name cards printed in Chinese. Although some Singaporeans adopt western given names, many are not familiar with how western family names are used. Often they will mistakenly address westerners by their given names, e.g. John Smith might be called "Mr John". In order to avoid confusion between given and family names, the family name is often underlined.

Meeting formalities

Names and forms of address

Singaporean Chinese assume Chinese names that are registered at birth. However, unlike their counterparts in China, they do not always use the *Hanyu pin yin* system (see Chapter 4, section on "Names and forms of address") in translating their names into the Roman alphabet. Instead, they use a direct English translation based on their spoken dialect, which in many cases resembles the *Hanyu pin yin* pronunciation. For instance, the *Hanyu pin yin* name Lin Li Zhu, is written in Hokkien as Lim Lay Choo. Chinese names in Singapore follow the Chinese custom where the family name appears first, followed by two given names.

The most common Singaporean Chinese family names are easy to pronounce, such as Tan, Tay, Teo, Yeo, Sim, Lee, Lim and Ong. Another common family name is Ng, pronounced with a nasal "ung" and using a short "U". The name Ooi is pronounced "wee".

For first meetings, a formal form of address using the family name (e.g. "Mr Tan") should be used, but fairly soon afterwards both first names can be adopted, e.g. Lim Gim Hai is addressed as "Mr Lim" on a first meeting , but is called "Gim Hai" on a less formal basis.

Sometimes a Chinese man will use the initials of his given names as a means by which he should be addressed, e.g. Lim Kam Chua may introduce himself as "KC" . Women do not follow this practice.

Many Singaporean Chinese also adopt a western given name in addition to their Chinese name. In this case, the western given name appears first, followed by the family name as applies in western circles. Women sometimes assume hybrids of western female names, such as Vanessia, Jaslyn, Karis, and Olinda, e.g. Karis Tan is formally addressed "Ms Tan", but once the acquaintance has been made, she may be called "Karis".

A western given name can be displayed together with a Chinese name, either at the beginning or end of the structure, in which case there will be four words. The western name is usually clearly distinguishable, e.g. Tay Tang Chye John (or John Yang Tang Chye) is informally called "John" in the western context and "Tang Chye" in Chinese.

Women do not take on their husband's name on marriage. Children are however given their father's family name. Women can either be addressed "Ms" or "Mrs" if they are married, and "Ms" if they are unmarried. Among the Chinese, an older woman may be addressed as "Madam", as a sign of respect.

As Malay names are quite different from those of ethnic Chinese and Indians, it is relatively easy to identify them. In Malaysia there are many complex forms of address and title applicable to Malays but, in Singapore, Malay names are comparatively simple. Their structure is based on a personal given name, followed by the father's given name:

{Own given name} {father's given name},
e.g. Mansor Rahmat.

The most notable feature is that family names are not used or passed down. Malays are usually addressed by the first given name that appears.

There are however different ways that this name can be expressed. Sometimes the word *bin* (male) or *binti/binte* (female) will be inserted between the two names. *Binte* is abbreviated to *bt* or *bte*. These small Arabic words mean respectively "son of" and "daughter of" the father whose given name appears at the end, e.g.: Mansor bin Rahmat – Mansor, son of Rahmat; or Haslina bt(e) Ibrahim – Haslina, daughter of Ibrahim.

To complicate matters further, some Malay women assume their husband's name, in which case *bte* will be excluded. In recent times some Malay women have begun adopting both their husband's and their father's names, in a hyphenated word.

In every day life, the Malay forms of address for Mr, Mrs and Miss apply to those who do not enjoy special status. These are respectively "Encik", "Puan" and "Cik", followed by their given name. In Malay, "C" is pronounced "CH", such that Encik is pronounced "enchik" and Cik is pronounced as "chik". The "U" in "UA" is pronounced like a "W" so that Puan is pronounced "pwunn". It is quite acceptable to address an unmarried female as Puan as this is also considered a sign of respect,

e.g.: Mansor bin Rahmat = Encik Mansor;
Haslina bt(e) Ibrahim = Puan Haslina.

In normal business circles in Singapore, it is possible to dispense with the use of "Encik" and "Puan" at a fairly early stage of the relationship, and simply use given names, as would be done in the West.

Indian names

Traditionally, like Malays, Hindu Indians do not use a family name. Indians of Islamic faith will have a Muslim name, similar to that of Malays.

A male Hindu will use the initial of his father's given name first, followed by his personal name. He will be known as Mr {personal name}, e.g. A Ramalingam will be called "Mr Ramalingam".

Long given names may be shortened for ease of pronunciation. The man in the above example may be called "Mr Ram", or simply "Ram" in less formal circumstances.

Indian females use the same system – their father's initial plus their personal name. When a woman marries, her father's initial is dropped and her husband's personal name added to her own name, e.g. Ms S Thiru marries Mr Patel, becoming Mrs Thiru Patel.

Indians originating from Melaka in Malaysia may also have Portuguese names which date back to the early colonial days, e.g. Alvaro Da Silva will be called Mr Da Silva.

Sikhs, Indians wearing turbans around their heads have a given name, followed by the word *Singh* (male) and *Kaur* (female). These are not family names, but Sikh identifiers. As with the Hindu faith, family names are not used among the Sikh community. On no account should Indian Sikhs be addressed as "Mr Singh" or "Ms Kaur".

To trace parentage, the descriptors *s/o* ("son of") and *d/o* ("daughter of") are used, together with the parents' given name, e.g. the man Rajen Singh, *s/o* Bhopinder Singh, is Rajen, son of Bhopinder. Rajen Singh will then be called "Mr Rajen Singh" in business circles, and "Rajen" in less formal circumstances. The married woman Baldeva *d/o* Kaur is called "Ms Baldeva Kaur". If Baldeva Kaur married Rajen Singh, she would be addressed formally as "Mrs Rajen Singh", and informally as "Baldeva".

Meeting and greeting

Normal western protocol applies when meeting Singaporeans, where a firm handshake can be used. Handshake greetings between members of the opposite sex are also quite normal, although men should not shake hands with a Malay woman. If the other party is Malay, only a limp handshake with the right hand is necessary.

Indian men and women normally use a western handshake when meeting members of the same sex. A man does not normally shake hands with an Indian woman, and a western woman should not offer her hand to an Indian man. In such cases, a nod of the head and a slight smile can be given.

In Singapore, name cards should be presented to Chinese, Indians and Malays using the two-handed technique, with the writing displayed the right way up for the recipient to read. If presenting to a Malay person, a more deferential way is to pass the card across with the right hand, using the left hand to support the right wrist. On no account should the card be presented with only the left hand.

Preliminaries

Meetings in Singapore usually start on time as most Singaporeans have tight and busy schedules.

The process of selecting seats at the back of a meeting room, facing the entrance, applies in Singapore.

Singaporeans are adept at making pre-business small talk in order to break the ice. As the country is a hub for many industries, including regional air travel, they are usually well travelled, and the hot topic of conversation will be recent travel stories. Stock phrases such as "So, how's business?" or "Travelling a lot lately?" will be asked. In replying to the former question, care should be taken not to be too boastful or bullish. Answers such as "OK" or "Not too bad" are appropriate. The Chinese will hesitate to answer that "Business is great", as superstition dictates that this could precipitate a change in fortune.

Negotiation etiquette

As is the Chinese custom, the senior member of the Singaporean team will do most of the talking. Junior members should not contradict or interrupt, and westerners should also adopt this custom. As Singaporeans are highly westernised when it comes to negotiations and discussions, meetings should proceed smoothly and efficiently. However, in the usual Asian manner, upfront or direct statements, particularly those of strongly negative views, should be avoided.

Meals and entertainment

Invitations

If a meeting has been scheduled before lunchtime there could be an impromptu invitation to lunch. Singaporeans consider this an important part of relationship-building, and therefore any such invitation should be accepted. No offence will be taken if a meal invitation is declined, provided a convincing excuse is given.

When extending a meal invitation to a Muslim, care should be taken to select a restaurant that serves *halal* food. Failing this, guests will be severely restricted in the food items they can order from the menu. It should also be established before meal arrangements are made for Indians whether they are Hindu, Muslim or vegetarian.

Food and drink

Singapore has a small landmass with no free space for agriculture, so almost all food products are imported. As it is a highly cosmopolitan country, Singapore has a wide range of cuisine. Being broadminded, most Singaporeans are sensitive to the needs of foreign visitors and may, when issuing an invitation, suggest either western or Chinese food. For evening meals, the chances are that Chinese cuisine will be proposed.

Local preferences for Chinese food in Singapore are:

◻ Hainanese chicken rice: Steamed rice with steamed or roast chicken.
◻ Chilli/pepper crab: Deep-fried crab, either whole or in pieces, with chilli or black pepper sauce.
◻ *Dim sum*: This light meal, which originated in Hong Kong, is recommended at lunch and comprises small portions of dumplings of pork and prawn.
◻ Steamboat: a social meal that the Chinese in Singapore particularly enjoy. A gas-heated bowl of boiling water and a hot plate are provided at the table, around which guests can sit and cook. Portions of vegetables, seafood and meat are selected from a buffet counter, and then cooked in the water or barbecued on the hot plate.

Fortunately, the Chinese in Singapore are averse to eating some of the more challenging and exotic food items consumed in China, but nonetheless there are a few local items that westerners may find difficult to stomach:

◻ Jelly fish: Served raw as a starter, cut into long strips.
◻ Red baby octopus: Served cold and whole, as a starter.
◻ Sea cucumber: White and rubbery, with a sharp taste.
◻ Chicken feet: Usually served steamed.
◻ Fish head: Served in a curry sauce. The fish eye is considered a delicacy.
◻ Pig's intestines: Served boiled, in soup.
◻ Shark fin: Served in soup.
◻ Abalone: Cut into chunks or strips.

For unappetising dishes that are shared, only small quantities need be selected. Singaporeans, many of whom spend a lot of time travelling around China, are sensitised to unpalatable forms of Chinese food, and hence are more understanding when westerners decline certain dishes.

While in the western environment the "white meat" or that away from the bone of chicken and fish is usually preferred, Chinese savour "dark meat" or that attached to the bone. Thus fish head is considered a delicacy.

Dessert is usually cut fresh fruit, although sometimes mango pudding (a kind of mango custard), sago pudding or red bean soup may be served, all of which are quite tasty. At outside eating venues, a fruit known as durian may be offered. This is a large fruit, similar in appearance and size to a large pineapple. The fruit has a strong, pungent and pervading odour, and a flesh that is pale yellow with a consistency of raw pastry. While this is a popular delicacy for Chinese Singaporeans, many westerners find its smell and consistency repulsive.

Malay food is also very common in Singapore, and in keeping with Islamic ways does not contain pork. The words *nasi* (meaning rice) and *mie* or *mee* (meaning noodles) appear in many menu items and provide a clue as to what the basis of the meal will be. *Mie* dishes will comprise noodles either "wet" in soup, or "dry" in a fried form. Most dishes tend to be spicy. Some of the most common are:

◻ *Nasi goreng*: Fried rice with prawns and vegetables, topped with a fried egg.
◻ *Nasi lemak*: Rice steamed with coconut milk, served with fried anchovies, peanuts, egg, cucumber and fried chicken or fish.

- *Nasi pandan*: Rice, served in a banana leaf.
- *Mie goreng*: Spicy fried noodles, made with vegetables, chopped chicken and seafood.
- *Mie reebus, mie siam* or *laksa*: Spicy soups of egg noodles, vegetables and egg, in a spicy gravy.
- *Kway teow*: A dish made from fried flat noodles, containing either beef or seafood and mixed local vegetables.

Other dishes containing chicken (*ayam*), fish (*ikan*), beef (*daging*) and squid (*sotong*) are quite popular:

- *Daging rendang*: Cubes of beef in a spicy sauce.
- *Ayam rendang*: Chicken pieces in a spicy sauce.
- *Ikan goreng*: A fish stew.
- *Sotong sambal*: Squid with curried sambals.
- *Satays:* The equivalent of kebabs made from chicken, lamb or beef, cooked on a charcoal grill. They are served with a peanut sauce, and chunks of raw onion, cucumber and *nasi putih* (steamed rice compressed into cubes).

Westerners generally find all these dishes tasty and enjoyable, although somewhat spicy. Desserts are usually quite simple, consisting of cut fruit like watermelon, papaya and pineapple.

Indian food may be vegetarian and, in the case of Hindus, beef in any form will be forbidden. Muslim Indians will of course not eat pork or any non-*halal* food. The most common variety is northern Indian cuisine, which while spicy, tends to have a more delicate flavour than the usual hot curries that are served in western countries.

Despite the fact that there is a local Singaporean brewery, beer, wine and spirits are expensive, owing to high excise duties. In normal society, alcohol consumption tends to be lower than that of other countries. As Singaporeans are generally quite health conscious, they prefer to drink fresh fruit juice or Chinese tea, especially during the day. Alcohol is consumed during evening meals or at *Karaoke* sessions. Red wine is usually preferred to white, because its colour symbolises prosperity and the perception that it is good for the heart. Women do not usually drink alcohol at business functions, and alcohol will also not be offered at Malay functions.

Chinese table etiquette

The format and protocols of a Chinese meal in Singapore are the same as those found in China. Diners are seated around a large circular table, with the most senior host and guest seated at the far side, facing the entrance to the room.

The most senior member of the guest delegation is seated to the right of the most senior host, with the next most senior guest seated on his left. Guests should wait to be allocated seats by their host.

The place-setting usually comprises a bowl for soup, rice or noodles, and a small plate on which to place selected food items. Chopsticks and a flat-based spoon are provided. If difficulty is being experienced with the chopsticks, it is permissible to pick up the flat spoon with the left hand (for right-handed people), push food onto the spoon using the chopsticks in the right hand, and to then eat from the spoon.

As in China, dishes are shared and not served as individual orders. A large number of dishes are placed in the centre of the table, from which diners may help themselves. Small portions are selected from the main dish, either with chopsticks or a serving spoon, and placed on individual eating plates.

At the beginning of the meal, a number of cold meat or vegetarian appetisers may appear, followed by soup, and then a series of hot dishes, finishing with rice or noodles. Soup is served throughout the meal into each diner's soup bowl, and then consumed using the flat-bottomed spoon. It is not polite to pick up the soup bowl and drink from it, as is done in Japan. Morsels of food in the soup may be picked out and eaten with the chopsticks or flat-bottomed spoon.

Fish, usually served whole, is divided into pieces at the table. The fish is placed on the table, with its head facing the guest of honour. It is considered bad luck to turn the fish over to access the meat underneath, as in the sailing or fishing environment this portends that a sailing vessel will capsize and sink. The tastiest part of the fish is the head – the eye is considered a real delicacy. The head is reserved for the most important guest, and may be served by the host as a sign of honour. The honoured guest is expected to partake of the flesh (the cheek) from the fish head. When chicken is served, the head of the chicken may also appear on the main serving dish. In this case, it is intended for decoration purposes only and should not be presented to anyone, as it will bring bad luck to them.

Rice or noodles are normally served near the end of the meal, just prior to dessert. These are considered "fillers" in case diners have not had enough to eat during the main meal.

Chinese table etiquette dictates that:

- Guests should allow the host to begin eating first, or for the host to invite them to begin eating.
- Pieces selected from the main dish should not be transferred directly to the mouth, without first being placed on the eating plate.
- Business should not be discussed during the meal. Such time should be used to nurture the relationship, by asking about family life.
- It is possible that the host will select some special morsel from the table and place it on a guest's plate; this is a sign of respect, for which thanks should be given. The morsel should be eaten.
- Morsels of food should not be selected from the main serving dish by "picking and hunting" with the chopsticks. The piece to be selected should be visually identified first, before it is taken from the dish.
- Food should not be piled up on the eating plate from the main serving dish.
- It is permissible from a seated position to stretch across the table to select food from a dish; however, it is considered impolite to stand and reach across the table.
- When reaching across to select something from the table, one's arm or chopsticks should not cross that of another person, as this creates an "X" which is a sign of death.

◻ Once a bite has been taken out of a selected piece of food, it should not be dipped back into a commonly shared dish of sauce.

◻ At the end of the meal, a small amount of food should be left on the plate, otherwise the host will continue to offer more food.

◻ The mouth should be covered with the hand, while using toothpicks to remove food particles from the teeth.

◻ Chinese *"ganbei"* toasting is not that common in Singapore. It is acceptable to sip alcohol as would be done in the West, without waiting for a toast.

◻ Singaporeans, on special evening occasions such as a wedding, may propose a toast at the end of the meal, by shouting *yam seng* after which they drain their glasses.

Once a meal is over, most Singaporean Chinese depart almost immediately.

Malay table etiquette

Malay meals are normally eaten with a spoon and a fork. The fork is held in the left hand, and the spoon in the right. The fork is used to push food onto the spoon, which is then used to transfer the food to the mouth. The traditional Malay way of eating is with the fingers, but this is not common in normal business circles. Dishes are normally placed in the centre of the table, and shared. Serving spoons are provided for each dish, and in such cases the right hand is used for serving with the spoon.

Malay table etiquette dictates that:

◻ The left hand should not be used to pass dishes or other items around the table.

◻ The American manner of using an upturned fork in the left hand, to shovel food into the mouth, is not considered polite in terms of Muslim table etiquette.

◻ The right hand should always be used for the transfer of food to the mouth.

Indian table etiquette

Indians sometimes eat with their hands, with food being eaten off a single cut banana leaf. A variety of dishes, sauces and condiments are served on the banana leaf, around a centrally placed pile of rice (*nasi daun pisang*). In this situation, dishes are not shared. When the meal has been completed, diners will be able to wash their hands at a basin located in an open area of the restaurant.

Table etiquette dictates that:

◻ Only the right hand should be used for transferring food to the mouth.

◻ It is considered impolite to suck or lick the fingers during the meal.

◻ Elbows should not be placed on the table.

◻ When the meal is over, the leaf should be folded in half towards the body. The leaf is only folded away from the body at a funeral meal, or if the meal was less than satisfactory.

Once a meal is over, most Singaporeans depart almost immediately.

Evening entertainment

In Singapore, everyone usually goes home once dinner is over, although it is possible for further entertainment to be suggested. The most common form of after-dinner entertainment is *Karaoke*, which can be enjoyed by both male and female participants. There is a wide range of *Karaoke* bars, those catering for men only, as well as for mixed-gender groups. Women visitors can therefore be included in invitations to *Karaoke*, although in business circles this tends to be mainly a male pastime. Establishments catering for men will usually offer hostesses, who serve drinks and may also sit with guests and sing along with them. In *Karaoke* bars serving mixed groups, waiters normally serve the drinks. Beer, whisky or soft drinks for women are usually served. As *Karaoke* in Singapore is an excellent way to develop business relationships, westerners should be prepared to accept such invitations and to participate in the singing.

There are a number of night spots in Singapore, where westerners might be entertained. The North Boat Quay and Clarke Quay areas along the diminutive Singapore River abound with bars and restaurants, and are popular places for gathering after work.

11 The Philippines

The Philippines, situated south of Taiwan and north of Borneo is an archipelago of 7 107 islands, only 11 of which are of any significance. The northernmost and largest island is Luzon, on which the capital Manila is situated. The central region is known as the Visayas, while Mindanao, the second largest island, is southernmost. The Spanish, who colonised the country during the 16th century, named it after the ruling Spanish king's son, Philip.

Philippine culture originates from Malaysia, China, Spain and America, creating a race (Filipino) that adapts easily to new environments. Filipinos thrive in foreign countries and are found working in many service-related industries around Asia, the Middle East and beyond. Philippine women, as a means of earning higher incomes can be found working as household maids around Asia. It is not surprising, therefore, that one of the Philippines largest "export" industries is its manpower.

As with most other south-east Asian countries, there is a small component of ethnic Chinese in the Philippines who dominate private business. As their ways are different from those of the Filipinos, western business people should be prepared to deal with two distinct cultural groups.

Country background

Population
The population of the Philippines is 85 million.

Ethnicity and religion
There are over 100 different tribes on the archipelago. During the 16th and 17th centuries, intermarriage between Spanish, Chinese and the local population created a breed known as *meztisos*. Any Spaniard born in the Philippines during the days of Spanish occupation was known as a "Filipino". Following later periods of American occupation, this term was extended to any citizen of the Philippines, including *meztisos*. Today, a male is known as a "Filipino" and a female as a "Filipina". Modern Filipinos sometimes refer to themselves as Pinoys (male) and Pinays (female), and comprise over 90% of the population. There is a small contingent of ethnic Chinese of Fukien descent, accounting for 2% of the population.

Over 90% of the population are Christian, being mainly Roman Catholic. The remainder are Protestant. Islam is practised mainly in the south by 5% of the population.

Language and script

There are over 70 different language groups in the Philippines, the dominant one being *Tagalog* ("tah-gah-log") which has Malay origins. The *lingua franca* is *Pilipino* (or *Filipino*), based mainly on *Tagalog*. The Roman alphabet is used in both *Tagalog* and *Filipino*, with word pronunciation similar to that of English. *Tagalog* and other Filipino dialects are spoken quite loudly and have a distinctive nasal "twang".

The country claims to be the third-largest English speaking population in the world, as well as having one of the highest literacy rates – in excess of 90%. Owing to the fact that all Filipinos are taught English as a primary language, most business with foreigners can easily be conducted in English.

There is a significant residual Spanish influence in the country, and some older Filipinos are able to speak the language. Many names and pronunciations are in Spanish. For instance: "J" is pronounced like an "H". The family name Bajacan is pronounced "Ba-ha-can".

"X" is also pronounced as an "H". The name "Roxas" is pronouced "Roh–has".

Filipinos have difficulty in pronouncing "F" and "V" sounds. Because of this they sometimes substitute "F" with "P", and "V" with "B". The letter "I", when contained in a syllable, is pronounced as an extended "EE". Thus the word fish may be pronounced "peesh" and fifty as "peepty".

Regional structures

There are 79 provinces grouped into 16 regions, each of which is headed by a governor. Each province comprises a number of *Barangays*, which are social units containing a nucleus of villages and smaller districts. The capital Manila, a large sprawling metropolis comprises 13 constituencies, collectively known as "Metro Manila".

Political environment

Since achieving independence in 1946, the country has functioned as a unitary republic, modelled on the American system. The president is elected by the nation, and serves a term of six years. Following the tyranny of the Marcos regime in the 1980s, it was constituted that any one president could serve only a single term and may not stand for re-election. Prior to the Marcos period, the president could run for two four-year terms.

There are two houses, a senate of 24 members also elected by the population, and a House of Representatives. This comprises 250 members (elected by citizens of the regional districts) who serve a term of four years.

The party system is a complicated one, based on coalitions and jostling of politicians for senior government positions. Gloria Arroyo, the current president, won the 2004 election under the umbrella of "K4", a coalition of Lakas (party of former President Fidel Ramos), The Liberal Party (Arroyo's own party), the Christian-Muslim Democrats (CMD) and the Nationalist People's Coalition (NPC).

Religious, cultural and historical influences

Catholicism, introduced by the Spanish during the 16th century, is the most dominant and widespread religion in the Philippines. Although many of the minority Chinese population follows Buddhist, Taoist and Confucian beliefs, some are also Christian. Islam is also practised, mainly on the island of Mindanao.

Ethnic boundaries

While the majority of the population is Filipino, a significant proportion of the minority Chinese population run their own enterprises, so that the probability of encountering Chinese people in business is high. It is possible to identify their ethnicity from their names. Their skin colour is lighter than that of Filipinos. Chinese in the Philippines are well integrated into local society, far more so than their counterparts in Malaysia and Indonesia.

Christianity

Christianity arrived with the Spanish immigrants in the 16th century. Over 80% of the population is Roman Catholic. The more devout consider themselves to be "God fearing" citizens and worship frequently. A further 10% of the population is Protestant or "free thinking". Two new Filipino church groups, the Aglipayan Church and Iglesia Ni Cristo, have recently emerged. The latter has become a powerful influence in both religious and political circles.

Islam

Malay traders introduced Islam with their arrival during the 10th century. There are two primary Muslim groups, the *Moros* and *Somal*, who are concentrated mainly in the south. Regrettably, this region has recently been subjected to violence at the hands of more radical Muslim sectors, such as the *Abu Sayff*.

Historical influences

Evidence found on the south-west island of Palawan suggests that man existed in the Philippines as long ago as 22 000 BC, and that early *homo sapiens* was able to survive the last ice age.

From 6000 BC, Indonesians and Negrito groups from the Malay peninsula and Borneo arrived. Malay groups began to prosper, leading to the development of a strong Muslim group, which later concentrated in the south of the archipelago.

Trade with China started in 1000 AD with good relationships developing between China and the Philippines. In 1952 the Spanish explorer Ferdinand Magellan landed on the Philippines. He was followed later by Miguel de Lopez de Legaspi, who was chiefly responsible for introducing Catholicism.

After nearly 200 years of Spanish rule, Britain invaded the capital, Manila, in an effort to expand the interests of the British East India Company, but handed it back two years later when a peace treaty was signed with Spain.

In 1898, following an American invasion (as a result of the American-Spanish war) the Spanish presence in the Philippines succumbed to American control. During World War II, Japan invaded the Philippines. The US resumed control again at the end of the War, granting the country its independence and installing the first Philippine president, Manuel Roxas, in 1945.

Between 1965 and 1982 the country was ruled by a harsh and corrupt president, Ferdinand Marcos, who murdered a large number of political activists. He imposed martial law and ruined the economy. He was finally ousted after a huge display of public dissatisfaction following election rigging.

Despite subsequent occasional periods of improved economic management, the Philippines has continued to suffer from poor governance at political levels. This has suppressed growth and done little to lift the majority of the population from abject poverty. The country continues to be at the mercy of a violent Islamic group located in the southern island of Mindanao, which from time to time makes its presence felt through bomb attacks at key locations.

Social and business values

It has been said that Filipinos are hybrids of Malays (in family values), the Spanish (in romance), the Chinese (in business) and the Americans (in ambition). Another interpretation cites a race that has lived for 400 years in a convent (under Spanish rule) and then 50 years in Hollywood (under American rule)! Thus a unique breed of God–fearing followers with American aspirations has evolved.

Despite an apparent shift towards western culture, Filipinos do have their own values, many of which are typically Asian. Thus westerners should not be misled by their American façade.

The Filipino identity or *asal* determines their code of conduct in society. Filipinos, like other Asians, abhor loss of face. They avoid *hiya*, or bringing shame on themselves, their kin, families and close associates. Because of this, *hiya* tends to be a controlling influence in society. A transgression or crime committed by an individual would result in social rejection of the perpetrator. In turn, this would harm the individual's *amor-propio*, or self-respect. Despite the so-called self-policing system of *hiya*, the Philippines is rife with bribery and corruption. The secret is not to be caught committing an impropriety! In order to avoid the risk of discovery, go-betweens or "fixers" are used to handle delicate situations. The manner in which bribes (*lagay*) are offered is managed through such a process.

There are three levels of association in Philippine society. The power that these wield in business and politics is immense, and should not be underestimated:

- The **family unit**, which may also include extended family, is the cornerstone of a support base for its members, be it financial, moral or psychological. Decisions are taken by the family unit as a whole, and not by individual members.
- The **kinship** includes both near and distant family members, as well as childhood friends and other close acquaintances. Such relationships come into play when the close family unit is not in a position to provide assistance. A good example of this is in the political arena, where those in a position of power exploit their

155

positions to advance kin in government circles. Many presidents, such as Cory Aquino, Fidel Ramos and Gloria Arroyo have had influential relatives promote their political careers.

◻ The ***barkada*** is a grouping of peers who maintain a high degree of interdependence. It may be a professional organisation or a street gang. A good standing in such a group is considered necessary for career growth and personal advancement.

To survive in these hierarchies, particularly the *barkada*, *pakikisama* is required – an ability to get along with and be accepted by others. This means sacrificing individual desires for the benefit of the group, and as such, earning the respect of other members. In such a society, favours are granted on the understanding that there will some form of future reciprocation. This system is known as *utang na loob* and can be likened to the Chinese *guanxi*.

Westerners are well accepted by Filipinos. Western men are called "Joe", referring to the days of occupation of the Philippines by American soldiers, who were named "GI Joe". The term *Amerikanos* or *Kanos* is also used to describe white foreigners. Unlike most other Asian countries, women in the Philippines enjoy greater equality in business and politics, and for this reason western women should experience no difficulty being accepted by the male business society.

Along with many other populations in developing countries of the south-east Asian region, local Filipinos believe that Caucasian westerners are very wealthy and therefore charge over-inflated prices in shops and stores. There is usually a two-tier system of pricing – the "local price" and a much higher "foreign price". To some extent this line of thinking also prevails in business.

A significant amount of business in the Philippines rests in the hands of the ethnic Chinese. These wealthy groups exist as an association whose objective is to support the government elite, to earn beneficial policy decisions. As occurs in other south-east Asian nations, the local Chinese are more diligent in their approach to business than the majority ethnic group, making them effective business partners.

Local customs and etiquette

Special beliefs

Western visitors to the Philippines should be aware of the following special beliefs:

◻ Many Filipinos have second or third wives, who may also have children by them.

◻ Filipinos are not time conscious – there is always "plenty of time".

◻ Loss of temper is seen as a severe social lapse.

◻ Senior or elderly people are expected to be humble in their demeanour.

◻ The eyes and mouth play a significant role in revealing non-verbal cues. They can also be used for pointing and indicating directions.

◻ Raising of the eyebrows is not a sign of annoyance. It is a sign that the meaning of a message has been understood.

◻ Situations of direct conflict are avoided.

◘ When conveying bad news or during conflict, Filipinos smile in an effort to reduce tension.

Etiquette

When interacting with Filipinos, **don't**:

◘ Beckon with a crooked index finger. In the Philippines this is a way of calling dogs. The standard Asian method of palm down and flapping the hand is preferable. Similarly, snapping of the fingers to gain someone's attention is considered extremely rude.

◘ Show irritation at poor rates of service. The Philippines is a developing country, and it does take longer to get things done.

◘ Tap your fingers on the table when impatient. In the Philippines this is interpreted as a sexual proposition.

◘ Use the western "OK" sign of making a circle with the thumb and forefinger, as this signifies money.

◘ Stand with arms akimbo and hands on hips. This is seen as a challenging stance.

◘ Show anger or shout in times of stress.

◘ Rebuke a Filipino in public.

◘ Initiate a discussion about the second-wife system of the Filipinos. While such a system is quite common in the Philippines, it is not openly discussed.

◘ Stare excessively. This is considered rude and a display of aggression.

◘ Show annoyance when a Filipino tries to attract your attention by quickly brushing his fingers over your elbow.

◘ Pound the fist into palm of the other hand as a sign of initiating action. Filipinos interpret this as a sign of aggression.

Preparation and awareness

Appointment scheduling

As most Filipinos have a good understanding of English and are familiar with American ways, they usually respond to written requests for appointments. The Filipino way dictates that invitations, particularly to social occasions, should be re-confirmed at least once and again the day before.

During the dry season, especially in May, many Filipinos return home to the rural areas to participate in fiestas, and therefore may not be available for appointments.

As the main business area of Metro Manila and other cities are notorious for traffic jams, extra time should be allowed for travelling between appointments. Traffic jams may be exacerbated during the monsoon season of July to September, when heavy rains are experienced. Exceptionally long delays occur during the extended Christmas period, which starts towards the end of November. During this time, the frequency of church and shopping mall visits increases, with the result that traffic grid-lock can be expected around these venues. It is not uncommon for travelling times to nearby destinations to vary between 30 minutes and three hours.

Although visitors are required to arrive on time for appointments, they should expect to be kept waiting by their hosts for fifteen to twenty minutes. Such delays mean that meetings may finish later than expected.

Gifts

There are only a few restrictions regarding gift-giving protocol in the Filipino world. Small gifts are generally well received, particularly items of food or an item from one's home country. The gift should not be too expensive as it could be perceived as a bribe. Once a business deal has been concluded, a more expensive gift may be given. When contact is made with ethnic Chinese businessmen, their etiquette of gift-giving will apply, where the following items should be avoided:

- ◻ Clocks (a sign that death is near).
- ◻ Knives, scissors or letter-openers (represents a severance of the relationship).
- ◻ Socks, sandals, handkerchiefs and towels (associated with funerals and grieving).
- ◻ Flowers, unless they are for the sick, for weddings or for funerals.

Gifts should be presented with either the right hand or with both hands. In the Philippines, it is a sign of greed if a gift is opened upon receipt. Thus, in the usual Asian custom, gifts are opened later.

Dress code

Clothes and form of dress are considered an important aspect of doing business in the Philippines. Although the local form of dress is relatively informal, westerners are still expected to dress appropriately. Men should wear a plain long-sleeved shirt with a tie; a jacket is not essential. In a less formal environment a tie is not really necessary. For more formal occasions, such as evening functions, a suit should be worn. Adventurous male visitors can adopt the local business attire, which consists of an open-neck, long-sleeved shirt with an embroidered design (*barong tagalog*) that is worn loose over trousers. This is extremely practical, being both cool and suitably formal. Women should wear knee-length skirts, and blouses with conservative necklines. Trousers should be avoided.

Name cards

As English is well understood, name cards as used in the western environment can be presented.

Meeting formalities

Names and forms of address

Filipinos use the western form of address, consisting of Mr, Mrs or Miss, followed by the family name. Given names can also be used at an early stage of a relationship. However, in Filipino society, as a sign of respect, an older or more senior person is addressed by their juniors as *Po*. Thus the word *O-Po* meaning "Yes sir/madam" may be applied to a senior westerner.

Most Filipino names are Hispanic in origin, using western name structures that comprise one or two given names followed by the family name. Given names are usually quite long, and are shortened to their western forms, e.g.: Mr Romelito Coruna would introduce himself as "Omer"; Mr Arturo Ramoz would be called "Art"; Ms Milagros Catoto would abbreviate her name to "Mila".

An abbreviation such as "Sta" or "Sto" may also appear in a Filippino name. These are the respective short forms of the names Santa and Santos.

The name Edilberto Sta Racelis in full, is written Mr Edilberto Santa Racelis. He would abbreviate his given name to "Ed".

Although married women usually assume their husband's family name, some in business circles continue to use their maiden name hyphenated with their husband's family name. In formal situations it is acceptable to use the maiden name, e.g.: Milagros Garcia-Agbayani would be called "Ms Garcia".

In professional circles, status is given to someone by using their title, as displayed on their name card, e.g. "Engineer Cruz" or "Attorney Cruz".

Ethnic Chinese usually have only two names. Their legal Philippine name is usually Spanish, followed by a short family name of Chinese origin, e.g.: Wilfredo Cy has a Chinese family name pronounced "See"; Antonio Go, Lucindo Teh ("Tay") and Nina Cua ("Chua") are also names belonging to ethnic Chinese.

Interpretation of names therefore provides useful clues to a person's origin and their etiquette. While most ethnic Chinese of the Philippines accept Filipino ways, favour will be gained if their particular customs are observed.

Meeting and greeting

The western way of greeting with a handshake is practised in the Philippines. A light grip is used. It is acceptable for women to shake hands with men, although men should wait for a woman to offer her hand. Similarly, a western woman should initiate a handshake with a Filipino male.

In their own society, Filipinos greet each other by establishing eye contact and raising their eyebrows. A traditional greeting with an elderly or senior person is for the more junior person to place the senior person's hand or knuckles on their forehead. Westerners are not expected to follow this custom.

Name cards are presented using both hands. In many cases Filipinos may not have name cards. If a card is not offered, requesting one may cause embarrassment to the person concerned.

Preliminaries

On entering a meeting room, guests should wait to be seated by the host. Seating arrangements are based according to hierarchy, with counterparts of the same level of seniority seated opposite one another. The most senior member of a delegation should be seated at the centre of his or her side of the table.

Negotiation etiquette

As time is not of the essence in the Philippines, much time may be taken up by small talk. Under such circumstances, westerners should not force the pace by interrupting or prematurely changing the topic of discussion to business matters. The Filipino party should be allowed to govern the pace of proceedings.

During discussions, the group terminology of "we", "us" and "our" should be used instead of the singular terms "I", "me" and "my".

Filipinos may at times appear to be excessively silent during discussions. They may not understand, or they may disagree with what is being said. To disclose either would be seen as causing loss of face, or initiating public conflict. More junior members of a Filipino team will keep silent, deferring to their seniors unless requested to contribute. It is considered polite to display a degree of humility and maintain a quiet demeanour.

To avoid conflict arising from disagreements, the Filipino way is to give an indirect negative response. Responses such as "we'll see", "let us come back you", "if you say so" imply "no". A negative response is also given by raising the eyebrows, without offering a comment. Westerners might interpret such replies as being far more positive than actually intended. In case it is necessary to contradict someone, this should be done in a discreet indirect way, or privately after the meeting.

There are times where it is necessary to ensure that Filipinos are committed to what has been agreed. This can be achieved by double-checking, and where possible obtaining a written confirmation. Although group decision-making (*pakikisma*) is important, decisions will usually be passed up through the hierarchy for a more senior person's approval.

Meals and entertainment

Invitations

Unlike most other Asian cultures, Filipinos have a tendency to entertain at their homes. Spouses are usually included in dinner invitations, but not in business lunches. Invitations extended to Filipinos for meals or functions should be issued in a suitably formal manner, preferably in writing. It is also recommended that follow-up telephonic contact at least once, if not twice immediately beforehand, be made to re-confirm their attendance.

Filipinos are notorious for not arriving for functions, even though they may have accepted an invitation. On the other hand, also expect them to arrive with an uninvited friend!

Ethnic Chinese will always be quick to issue lunch or dinner invitations because, like their south-east Asian counterparts, they use mealtimes for relationship-building. Spouses will not usually be included.

Food and drink

Filipino food is a mixture of Malay, Chinese and Spanish cuisine. Because of the different subcultures spread across the archipelago, many different kinds of cuisine can be found. Filipino food is not normally spicy, except for that of the Visayas in the south. There are a few Filipino specialities that foreigners may have difficulty with:

- *Balut*: A duck's egg, where a half-formed duckling is eaten whole out of the shell. Fortunately this is not served in too many restaurants and tends to be confined mainly to streetside food stalls.
- *Bagoong*: A salty paste of small shrimps and vinegar, which has a strong taste and aroma. This is used as a dipping sauce for meat and vegetables.
- *Chicharon*: Fried pig's intestine.

Hosts will understand if western guests politely decline to partake of these, provided no visual show of disgust is given. There are fortunately several Filipino dishes that are quite tasty, and well worth a try:

- *Adobo*: A stew of chicken or pork in a vinegar, soy and garlic sauce.
- *Bulalo* soup: Soup of beef and cabbage.
- *Sinigang*: A sweet-and-sour vegetable soup
- *Caldereta*: A beef stew.
- *Apritada*: Pork or chicken, served in a tomato sauce.
- *Kare Kare*: A stew of eggplant, French beans and pork in a peanut sauce.
- *Lechon de leche*: A vestige from the Spanish days. This is a small pig, roasted whole and carved at the serving table. It is usually encountered at fiestas or special occasions.
- *Pinakabet*: A mixture of vegetables, such as eggplant, okra and pumpkin, in a shrimp paste.
- *Pancit*: Noodles, fried with either meat or vegetables, in the Chinese way.

Although most Filipino menus are written in English, in more remote areas this may not be the case. It is therefore useful to know the following *Tagalog* words for common forms of food:

- *Manok*: chicken.
- *Baka*: beef.
- *Baboy*: pork.
- *Isda*: fish.
- *Hippon*: prawns.
- *Panos*: squid.

As Filipinos have a sweet tooth, desserts constitute an important part of the meal. Two desserts well worth trying are:

- *Ubi*: A purple-coloured ice cream, produced from the *ubi* yam.
- *Halo halo*: A parfait glass of fruit preserve, corn kernels, beans, jelly cubes and sago, with coconut milk and crushed ice.

Alcohol is not always freely consumed at meals. While beer or wine is usually offered to men, it is expected that women should not consume alcohol. There are two local alcoholic brews in the Philippines. *Basi* is a port-like wine made from sugar cane, and *Lambanog* is a spirit made from coconut juice. The alcohol content of both these beverages is quite low.

Local fruit drinks include calamansi juice, squeezed from a small green citrus fruit similar to a lime. It has a tart taste that can be sweetened by adding sugar syrup. *Buko* juice is coconut milk that contains pieces of white coconut flesh.

Table etiquette

It is considered polite to arrive fifteen minutes late for a meal, as Filipinos believe that arriving on time displays a sign of greed. When Filipinos entertain at home, guests are expected to bring a gift of flowers or a small delicacy.

The table setting is usually a circular table with a revolving centre section on which shared dishes are placed. The menu is likely to be a three- or four-course meal, starting with soup, followed by two or three courses, ending with dessert. Rice is always consumed with Filipino cuisine. It is placed in the centre of each diner's plate, usually in the form of a moulded shape from a small serving bowl. Guests help themselves from the main serving dish, placing their helpings alongside the rice mound on their plates.

In wealthier domestic environments wine may be served with a meal, otherwise water and soft drinks are usually provided.

Guests should wait for the host to invite them to begin eating – it is a sign of greed to commence eating immediately.

Food is eaten with a spoon and a fork. The spoon and not the fork is used to transfer food from the plate to the mouth. The fork is for pushing items of food onto the spoon. The spoon can also be used to cut up larger pieces of food.

Correct table etiquette dictates that:

◻ At the end of a course, it is considered polite to leave a small amount of food on your plate.

◻ If there is a need to ask the way to the toilet, it is useful to know that in the Philippines this is referred to as a "comfort room", or by its acronym "CR".

◻ It is customary when dining at a host's house for any leftover food to be offered to guests to take away with them. This custom flows from the ancient tradition of *pabalon*. It is considered impolite to refuse such a gesture.

◻ On no account should a female host be addressed or referred to as a "hostess", as done in western society. In the Philippines this word refers to a prostitute.

◻ Caution should be exercised when passing a compliment about the cooking ability of the lady of the house. In many Filipino homes, a maid undertakes preparation of the meals.

Evening entertainment

As Filipinos enjoy singing, time may be made available after dinner for *Karaoke*. If alcohol is served during singing sessions, care should be taken not to become excessively drunk. Filipinos expect westerners to behave with dignity.